FRANK LLOYD WRIGHT

GENIUS!
The Artist and the Process

FRANK LLOYD
WRIGHT

BY

WENDY BUEHR MURPHY

GENIUS!
The Artist and the Process

SILVER BURDETT PRESS

Created and produced by: Blackbirch Graphics, Inc.

Project Editor: Emily Easton
Designer: Cynthia Minichino
Cover Design: Leslie Bauman

Manufactured in The United States of America

10 9 8 7 6 5 4 3 2 1

Library of Congress Cataloging-in-Publication Data

Murphy, Wendy B.
  Frank Lloyd Wright / by Wendy B. Murphy.
  p. cm. — (Genius!: the artist and the process)
  Includes bibliographical reference (p.).
  Summary: Follows the life of the architect whose innovative designs revolutionized his field.
  1. Wright, Frank Lloyd, 1867-1959—Juvenile literature. 2. Architects—United States—Biography—Juvenile literature. [1. Wright, Frank Lloyd, 1867-1959. 2. Architects.] I. Title. II. Series: Genius! (Englewood Cliffs, N.J.) NA737, W7M85 1990 720'.92—dc20
[B] [92]
ISBN 0-382-09905-2 (lib. bdg.)   90-30557
ISBN 0-382-24033-2   CIP
                                   AC

(*Frontispiece*)
Frank Lloyd Wright broke the barriers of conventional architectural thinking, giving human society a new version of the form and function of the built environment.

Contents

*Primarily, Nature furnished the materials
for architectural motifs out of which the
architectural forms as we know them today
have been developed, and, although our
practice for centuries has been for the most
part to turn from her...and adhere slavishly
to dead formulae, her wealth of suggestion
is inexhaustible; her riches greater
than any man's desire.*
–Frank Lloyd Wright

CHAPTER 1

A CHILDHOOD OF HAPPINESS AND SORROW
1867-1886

As June 8, 1867, dawned in the small farming community of Richland Center, Wisconsin, there was a fair amount of commotion in the tiny house belonging to William and Anna Wright. William paced nervously in the hallway outside the bedroom where his wife lay.

Finally, after what seemed to him an eternity, the village doctor came out of the bedroom, wiping his hands on a towel. He clapped William's shoulder, smiled, and said, "Happy news, Mr. Wright! It's a boy, and both mother and child are fine, just fine!" The newborn was none other than Frank Lloyd Wright, though in his first months he carried the name

Frank Lincoln Wright, the name "Lincoln" being conferred on him by his father in honor of the recently assassinated President.

Frank's American ancestry was long and deep, tracing its roots back to the early seventeenth century, when the first generation of Wrights arrived in the colonies from Yorkshire, England. Grandfather David Wright, a Baptist minister, had distinguished himself as a preacher in Hartford, Connecticut, and father William Cary Wright, born in 1825 during Thomas Jefferson's presidency, had grown into young manhood in and around Connecticut's capital city.

William, Frank Lloyd Wright's father, came to maturity during a time that saw the American nation grow on a grand scale. Much of this growth was brought about by men who were willing, even eager, to exploit both the land and other people. But William Wright's temperament went more toward serving his fellow man, an attitude that undoubtedly contributed to his lifelong financial struggles.

William Wright pursued his goal of human service first in medicine and then in legal studies. But in each case he was dissatisfied with the gross imperfections he saw in his intended profession. It was only when he entered the ministry, following in his father's footsteps, that he finally felt emotionally fulfilled. Ordained a Baptist minister in 1863, he would serve many congregations during his life, in the process changing his church affiliation to Unitarian.

When William was twenty-six and barely out of college, he married Permelia Holcomb, a young woman from Litchfield, Connecticut. In time they moved to Lone Rock, Wisconsin, following the great westward migrations of the era. While they supplemented the family finances by taking in boarders, William also earned extra money as an accomplished musician and orator, giving rousing performances at funerals and patriotic celebrations alike. The young couple were on their way to raising three children when Permelia died of childbed fever, a common cause of death for women of those days. Left with the responsibility of raising three youngsters, William badly needed a wife and mother for his children. So it came as no surprise to townsfolk when he soon declared his intention to marry Anna Lloyd Jones, a pretty young schoolteacher who boarded with the family.

Anna, Frank's mother, was born in Wales, Great Britain, in 1839. She was brought to America at the age of six by her parents, who followed others in the large Lloyd Jones clan in search of a better life. The Joneses were quite successful in this quest; four of Anna's five brothers founded large, prosperous farms in a valley near Spring Green, Wisconsin. The fifth brother, Jenkin Lloyd Jones, was a prominent Unitarian minister. Admired as they all were, they must have been a bit off-putting in their self-confidence and self-congratulation, for they were known among some of the other townspeople as "The God-Almighty Joneses."

Like her brothers, Anna was broad-shouldered, strong, and uncommonly tall—several inches taller than her husband, William. She was also very strong willed, and perhaps because she came from a very tightly knit, ambitious family, she found it difficult to tolerate William's restlessness and inability to commit himself to a profession. She also seems to have had difficulty relating to people generally, for she was somewhat bookish and socially withdrawn.

Before her marriage to William and during the first months afterwards, Anna must have made a great effort to overcome her natural personality, for she was said to have been friendly enough toward her new stepchildren, Charles, George, and Elizabeth. This made the children happy, for they very much missed having a mother, and they naturally hoped that Anna would do her best to fill that empty place.

Soon, however, it became clear to William and the youngsters that their relationship with Anna was going to be difficult at best. Anna apparently found her own ambitions stifled in marriage, but in those days there was no easy way for a headstrong, artistic woman to express herself outside the home. Frustrated and angry, she became increasingly hostile, and even physically abusive, demonstrating what the Lloyd Joneses described as her "most tremendous temper." She beat the children when they displeased her and nagged them constantly.

Many years later Elizabeth recalled her stepmother's abusive behavior:

> One time in the winter when Mother was in one of her tantrums, she got mad about something and as usual vented it on me; she jumped up and down and pumped water as fast as she could and threw it over me and yelled with every jump. Father had his study on the third floor but he heard the racket and came down to see what was up. He told me to go upstairs but I was afraid to go past her to the stairway and my clothes were dripping wet.... I slipped out the front door and went around to the back and up the outside stairs. My clothes froze on me before I could get in the house.

> One other time when he was home and up in his study, she was frying meat at the stove with a long two-tined fork that goes with a carving set. She got at me for something or nothing and grabbed me by the hair and held my head back and jabbed that fork at my face and said she would put my eyes out. I screamed, "Papa!" with all my might and he came running down and stopped her, but I had the worst fright of my life.... I never could please her, no matter how hard I tried. She admitted sometimes that she hated me and all my relatives; she said she would like to have all our heads laid over a log, and she would take an ax and chop them off. I don't know whether her mind was just right or not....

Anna Lloyd Wright (*left*) was a terror to all her children except her eldest son Frank (*right*), on whom she showered all her affections.

Apparently, Anna did not reserve her anger for her stepchildren alone. She also was said to attack her husband from time to time, striking out at him when she could not contain her temper. In hopes of keeping the peace, Charles, George, and Elizabeth were eventually sent to live with their Holcomb relatives, and for years afterward they saw little of their father and kept in touch largely through letters.

As the years passed, Anna even neglected Frank's younger sisters, Jane and Maginal, born two and eleven years after him. To the extent that Anna could give affection, she chose to lavish it entirely on her son and first-born. As if to establish whose son he really was, she changed Frank's middle name. Instead of Frank Lincoln, he was renamed Frank Lloyd, after her own side of the family. Frank, for his part, apparently accepted his princely position without qualms, setting himself off from the other children from an early age.

Because of his mother's intense adoration of him, combined with his father's growing separation from the household, Frank was inclined to see his mother as the source of everything important and admirable in his life and his father as an unloving near-stranger. But the truth as others saw it was that William had a considerable impact upon Frank, and most especially in their common love of music. Though Frank never attained the skill as a musician that his father did, he could play the viola and piano well enough to join in family musicales. And he understood the principles of musical composition sufficiently to see what composers like his father's beloved Bach and Beethoven were aiming for in their work.

Over his very long life Frank Lloyd Wright would frequently compare his goals as an architect to that of a musician, and he thought of music as "an edifice . . . of sound", or as another great nineteenth century figure had said, "frozen architecture." Artistry in both, he observed, depended upon the composer's sense of rhythm and balance, of themes and variations on those themes.

Frank also seems to have inherited his father's flair for fancy dressing, as well as his passion for reading and philosophy, his disinterest in the practical side of life, his wanderlust, and his gift for florid speech. Later in life, he would affect the grandiose manner of referring to himself in the third person "he" rather than in the first person "I." He wrote his autobiography in the third person. Frank would also follow his father's model in the distant relationship with his own children in the years to come.

Between 1869 and 1878 the Wright family moved four times as William accepted ministries in several different communities. During three of those years they were back east in Massachusetts, where William served Baptists in the small town of Weymouth, twelve miles from Boston. Anna found these years in the unfamiliar surroundings of New England even more intolerable and lonely than life in the Midwest had been, and perhaps to distract herself she began investigating ways to instruct her young son, whom she was quite convinced was destined for greatness.

Visiting Philadelphia's Centennial Exposition of 1876, Anna discovered among the displays in one of the halls a set of Froebel toys. These toys were named after Friedrich Froebel, a German teacher who founded the "kindergarten" method of teaching young children.

Froebel invented sets of geometric blocks and other imaginative toys using colors, textures, beads, strings, and folded paper as part of a system for early childhood learning through creative play. With the toys—some of them flat pieces, some round, and some rectangular—children were encouraged to experience all kinds of two-dimensional and three-dimensional relationships.

Anna seized upon Froebel's theories, visited kindergartens established in New York and Boston, and then set about teaching Frank to use the toys. Though he was nine at the time, and older than the kindergartners for whom the system was intended, he took to the blocks with delight and later credited his command of colors and form to his Froebel experience.

Here, from Frank's *Autobiography*, is his recollection of the Froebel method:

> The strips of colored paper, glazed and "matt," remarkably soft brilliant colors. Now came the geometric byplay of those charming checkered color combinations! The structural figures to be made with peas and small straight sticks: slender construction, the joinings accented by the little pea-green globes. The smooth shapely maple blocks with which to build, the sense of which never afterwards leaves the finger: *form* becomes *feeling* . . . . What shapes they made naturally if only one would let them!

No one can say for sure just what influence the toys and games really had on the future architect, but there is no question that Frank Lloyd Wright would always demonstrate a remarkable ability to think in three dimensions.

A year after Anna's trip to Philadelphia, the Weymouth church fell on hard times, and William once again found himself faced with the prospect of having to move on. During the summer of 1878, the Wrights settled in Madison, Wisconsin, a quiet farming community located a forty-mile train ride away from Spring Green and the Lloyd Jones family. At this time, William joined the Unitarians with the help of his brother-in-law, Jenkin Lloyd Jones, a prominent figure in the Chicago church and one of the directors of the western missions.

Frank later took these many moves and changes of affiliation as symptoms of his father's failure. But the reports of those outside the family who knew William suggest that he was greatly admired by his congregations, that they had come "to expect something original, practical, and unhackneyed" whenever he spoke, and that his decision to move on each time was always met with regret by those who had to bid him good-bye. Perhaps the elder Wright was kept moving by his lonely search for greater fulfillment, a characteristic that his son would share.

Once the family was back in Wisconsin, Anna saw to it that Frank spent lots of time with his Lloyd Jones relatives. Starting when Frank was eleven, he spent five summers working on his Uncle James' farm in Spring Green. Here, in order to harden his body and mind, Frank was required to rise each day before dawn and work hard at such chores as milking, haying, and shoveling out the barn.

At the time Frank so strongly disliked farm life that he once ran away. But in later years he wrote affectionately of the quiet order of the country life he had experienced on the farm, as compared with the disorderly tension of cities. And when he became a man and could choose where he wanted to live, he chose to settle back in these same beautiful hills and valleys, surrounded by the farms and fields he had worked as a boy. Wright, however, did manage to avoid the dirty work of running a farm. He always saw to it that others did the manual labor while he watched.

Meanwhile, Frank was proving to be an indifferent student in school. Although he was a voracious reader, his grades were barely passing.

If he showed little interest in formal school, he had all sorts of other interests. When the Wright family settled in Madison, Frank and a friend operated a small printing press in the basement of the Wright home, turning out crudely done greeting cards for family and friends. The layout, design, and composition work involved in this amateur enterprise would later serve him well in his architecture. He also liked to "invent" things, was forever experimenting with kites and other boyhood manufactures, and got into his share of mischief.

In 1885, before graduation, Frank decided to quit high school for good. He found it difficult to conform to the rules and regulations, saw no use for what his teachers were trying to teach him, and was almost certainly upset by what was going on at home. That spring, after nineteen years of unhappy marriage, William Wright filed for divorce from Anna.

All his life Frank held single-mindedly to his mother's version of how the couple's marriage came to an end; she claimed that his father had deserted her to escape his responsibilities, leaving her "deeply grieved, shamed" and wholly innocent of any role in the breakup. Wright wrote in his autobiography that his father's dissatisfaction stemmed from his jealousy over his son's relationship with his mother. "There was no longer much agreement between father and mother." Wright said his mother adored him and "... father ... was deep into learning to read Sanskrit. Mother for some years had been ailing. Poverty pinched."

Doubtless, Frank's growing hostility, coupled with the fact that William, ordinarily a strong disciplinarian, was no longer a physical match for the unruly Frank, did indeed contribute to his decision. That fact became very clear to both of them one day when Frank was sixteen and William undertook to thrash Frank for some infraction. It had happened in the stable and the young rebel got his father down on the floor and held him there until his father promised to let him alone. He had grown too big for that sort of thing. "Father ought to realize it," said the boy, as he went into the house, white, shamed, and shaken, to tell his mother.

Yet, even with the space between them growing into a chasm, Frank had to admit that he had a certain sympathy for the man. He wrote in his autobiography, "Something of that vain struggle of superior talents with untoward circumstance that was ... father's got to [me], and [I] was touched by it—never knowing how to show Father. Something—you see— had never been established that was needed to make [us] father and son. Perhaps the father never loved the son at any time."

Elizabeth Wright, Frank's older stepsister, had another explanation for why her father had finally decided on divorce, a particularly difficult decision in the more conservative nineteenth century, when divorce was rare at best and virtually unheard of for a minister. According to Elizabeth, William went to have a talk with his older children about what he should do. His second wife, he told them, ignored her duties as a mate and mother, insulted him constantly, and was dangerously extravagant with their limited funds.

At a family conference, William consulted with his oldest son, George, and Elizabeth and her fiancé, John Heller. Heller told his future father-in-law that he should get out, no matter what. "It was bad enough," he said, "to run the risk of hell in the next world without living in hell in this one." George urged his father to join him in his law practice, but William chose to go his own way. When the divorce was finally settled, Anna got the home in Madison and their three children. According to Elizabeth, William "started out for himself with nothing but his violins and a few other things."

In any case, William left town immediately after the divorce was granted, and Frank never saw him again.

With no father to support the family, Frank took a job as a draftsman in the office of William Conover, a civil engineer for the city of Madison. A civil engineer's job is to design and supervise the construction of public utility buildings and other projects. As a draftsman, Wright's job was to make precisely scaled "mechanical drawings" or blueprints of various systems and structures—the city water supply, roadways, rail lines, bridges, and buildings—that served the city and region. The drawings, with their precise measurements, were used by engineers and builders when they were constructing and repairing parts of the system.

Apparently Wright was a talented employee, for he was soon earning $35 per month. And, with Conover's encouragement, he began attending classes at the University of Wisconsin in Madison. Conover, "a cultivated and kindly man" by Frank's description,

Frank Lloyd Wright attended college at the Madison campus of the University of Wisconsin.

was also dean of the school of engineering at the university, and he was able to bend the rules a little to make room for his assistant, who lacked the required high school diploma. Engineering training was the best and perhaps the only way for Frank to pursue his chosen profession—to be an architect.

The decision had been foreordained by his mother, even before he was born. Writing in his autobiography, he explained that during her months of pregnancy, she had known that she was going to have a boy and that he would build beautiful buildings. "Faith in prenatal influences was strong in my mother. Fascinated by buildings, she took ten full-page wood engravings of the old English cathedrals from *Old England*, a pictorial periodical to which . . . father had subscribed, had them framed simply in flat oak and hung them upon the walls of the nursery." Anna intended her son to be an architect before he was born.

It was not many years after Frank's birth that he, too, believed architecture was his destiny, and he always seemed to share his mother's confidence that he would not only be good at it, but he would be "the best the world would ever know."

For a woman with great aspirations for her son, architecture was an odd choice at that time, for the field was then barely recognized as a profession. Indeed, in the entire United States, there were just four universities offering specialized training in architecture—Massachusetts Institute of Technology and Yale in New England, the University of Chicago in the Midwest, and Cornell University in New York. The University of Wisconsin and the majority of other large institutions offered architecture courses only as a part of engineering training. In most instances, the teaching of architecture was nothing more than the teaching of exterior decoration.

The majority of building in this country, and in Europe for that matter, was carried out according to stylistic traditions and techniques that differed very little from those of the Greeks and Romans. Structural theory was devoted to the possibilities of what was known as "post-and-lintel" construction, in which a series of vertical *posts* would be set to support *lintels*, or horizontal beams, and together they would form the skeleton of walls and the support for sheltering roofs. The heights and widths of the posts and lintels was determined not by the purpose of the building so much as by the structural capability of the materials, which were most often wood but which might also be stone or brick held together for stability.

When a new building was needed, most people were inclined to pick out a familiar looking example in an architectural pattern book and hire a skilled builder—a local artisan—to copy it more or less exactly, down to the decorative details that tradition required.

Few if any of these architects ever questioned whether there might be a better source of architectural ideas than pure imitation, and few wondered whether a democratic way of life might be more appropriately represented with some newer homegrown American style. It was presumed that all the best styles had already been designed and that the architect's job was to figure out which of these old styles best fit the needs of the present.

Also contributing to the general lack of experimentation that characterized architecture throughout most of the nineteenth century was the fact that the building types required by society were relatively few, and their specific engineering requirements already solved. Most people still lived in individual houses, as they always had. Most artisans still made and sold their wares in small shops that were similar in form to their houses, with small rooms and smaller windows. Most manufacturing enterprises occupied factory spaces that were just bigger versions of houses and shops. And most buildings stood in small- to medium-sized towns where there was plenty of space around each building to let it stand separately.

Any changes that an architect might make were more likely to be in matters of decoration—a slight change in the proportions of the windows, a different sort of cornice to trim the doors, an extra story or two. When young Wright came along, even such novel buildings as apartment houses, railroad stations, and office buildings were being built as though they presented no new challenges to the architectural imagination.

Since the University of Wisconsin offered no architectural courses, Frank studied a mix of engineering, literature, and languages. As in high school, he was a poor student. He later chalked up his poor performance to his unhappiness at home. His years at the university he said had been a time of "unfulfillment, dull pain, frustration, and unsatisfied longing." Frank stayed for a year and a half of the four-year degree program, but then his resistance to authority, his independence of mind, and his unusual certainty that he knew more than others got the best of him. Now just twenty years old, he decided it was time to strike out on his own. He would go to Chicago.

The streets of Chicago at the turn of the century bustled with commerce. The city held great expectations for the young, aspiring, and ambitious Frank Lloyd Wright.

CHAPTER 2

PROFESSIONAL BEGINNINGS
1887-1899

Frank Lloyd Wright's decision to move to Chicago in 1887 was only logical. The city offered incomparable excitement and opportunities for a young architect. A series of unique circumstances had created a city like no other in the world at that time. On its way to becoming the metropolitan center of the Midwest, with a population that had rapidly swelled to 300,000, this young metropolis on the shores of Lake Michigan was a hub of shipping and railways. Scores of brash new industries made their home there, as did hundreds of successful business leaders who were eager to give steel-and-stone witness to their financial achievements by erecting handsome office buildings and fine houses for themselves.

Just when the city reached a position of national importance, it was all but destroyed in the Great Fire of 1871, said to have been caused by a Mrs. O'Leary's cow kicking over a kerosene lamp. In the decades that followed, all energies were focused upon rebuilding a bigger and better city as fast as possible.

With so many huge challenges before it, Chicago's architects and engineers had to look at the city as they never had before. One thing was apparent—a city was not just a big village. It needed buildings that were designed specifically for an urban environment, where people lived crowded together on streets that were laid out in regular four-square grid arrangements. Chicago's builders also recognized that they had no time to construct new buildings in the classic revival style favored in the East for public buildings. The stonework and decoration that had been traditionally used was simply too time consuming for their clients. They had to look for new solutions to building.

Out of this necessity was born what came to be known as the Chicago School, a community of innovative architects who turned their backs on what architects were doing in the older cities of America along the Eastern seaboard and proceeded to come up with many astonishing new concepts in building. In less than a decade, these practical-minded pioneers made a direct attack on conventional design thinking for large-scale, commercial buildings, buildings constructed for business, industry, and public housing.

Taking their cues from the world of science and industry rather than from art, they mastered the technique of riveted steel framing, so that the interior framework of buildings could be assembled on site from factory-or foundry-produced structural parts in a matter of months instead of years.

Architects of the Chicago School were also innovative in the ways they thought about buildings from the inside out rather than from the outside in. When designing a building they considered such practical aspects as who would live and work inside these buildings and how they would use the spaces. Hard as it is to imagine today, most buildings in the past had been erected first, and only afterwards did their occupants figure out how to fit themselves and their activities inside.

A contemporary Chicago journal explained approvingly that the new style had been called into life by "the business principles of real estate. . . . Light, space, air, and strength were demanded . . . as the first objects of architectural design and ornamentation the second." The journal went on to say that these buildings were the first examples of "truly American architecture." Most critics since that time have tended to agree.

The names of the chief figures in the Chicago School soon became known well beyond the city's limits. First among them was William LeBaron Jenney, whose ten-story Home Insurance Building, completed in 1885, is generally regarded as the world's first skyscraper. Henry Hobson Richardson, who had studied architecture in Paris and had first made a name for himself in the East as an architect in the old-fashioned or "beaux arts" tradition, was also in Chicago, having come in 1885 to build a huge, wholesale department store for Marshall Field. Once there he adapted his style to Chicago's new mood, producing a building that was notable for the way it combined simple, efficient engineering with a natural grace and good looks. And there were other notables like Daniel Burnham, J.W. Root, Louis Sullivan, and Dankmar Adler, all of them engaged in a new kind of creative invention.

In deciding to go to Chicago, Wright surely knew that he was embarking on a great learning experience.

Wright's plans did not, however, meet with his mother's approval. Anna feared for Frank's safety in the big city, and his uncle, Jenkin Lloyd Jones, who was a prominent Unitarian minister in the city, was of the same opinion. "On no account let the young man come to Chicago," he wrote his sister. "He should stay in Madison and finish his education. That will do more for him than anything else. If he came here, he would only waste himself on fine clothes and girls."

Frank was very angry at these objections to his plans. He felt he was old enough to make up his own mind, and so decided to run away without telling anyone. He sold some rare old books that his father had left behind and bought a train ticket for Chicago. A very self-confident young man, he was eager to test his strengths in the world—and very anxious to get out from under his mother's constant watchful supervision.

Upon arriving in Chicago, the high-spirited young man found the city everything he had hoped it would be and more. The wide-eyed country boy saw his first electric lights and his first cable-drawn trolley car. And no sooner had he arrived than he spent one of his seven remaining dollars, all he had for buying food and lodging, to attend a ballet performance at the Chicago Opera House. This easy recklessness with money, a lifetime characteristic of his, was summed up in one of his favorite sayings: "Take care of the luxuries and let the necessities take care of themselves."

When it became apparent to Frank's Chicago uncle that the young man could not be turned back, Jenkin Lloyd Jones reversed himself and decided to help. He introduced young Wright to J. Lyman Silsbee, an architect who also happened to be in Jones's Unitarian congregation. Silsbee's firm had designed Jones's new church, and while the architect was not particularly original, he was a brilliant sketcher and early follower of H.H. Richardson. Silsbee's commissions were of the residential, or house, variety rather than commercial, and in emulating Richardson, he took his inspiration from the master's so-called "Shingle Style," shingle-covered houses with wide, overhanging roofs, picturesque turrets, and deep-set, wrap-around porches.

Wright liked working at Silsbee's, but he left the firm after a few months, feeling he had learned all that was possible from his employer. His job there was limited to doing architectural detailing, that is, sketching in the finishing ornamental touches on buildings that were totally conceived and developed by Silsbee. Wright also wanted more money, so he went with the powerful Chicago firm of W.W. Clay. But here, with his still limited training, Wright soon realized that he was out of his depth. He returned briefly to Silsbee, who gave him a small raise. But he was still restless and soon left again.

Wright next joined the celebrated firm of Adler & Sullivan as a draftsman, just as they were in the midst of designing the Auditorium Building, at the time the single largest building that had ever been commissioned in the United States, and one whose fine design would soon make them famous. The new job proved to be one of the most important decisions of his young life, for Wright was now in the daily company of men whose personalities and abilities would influence him for the rest of his career.

Two more dissimilar bosses than Dankmar Adler and Louis Sullivan would be hard to imagine. German-born Adler was a self-taught, somewhat methodical engineer, whose first experiences with building had been gained during service in the Union Army. Never creative on his own, his talents for business, his

Louis Sullivan's Auditorium Building (1887-1890) emulates
H.H. Richardson's bold style of architecture.

deep understanding of engineering principles, and his
generally agreeable nature made him an essential part
of his firm's remarkable success over the years.

Louis Sullivan, by contrast, was a brooding, emotionally unstable "outsider." Raised in Boston, he
enrolled at the Massachusetts Institute of Technology
(M.I.T.) to study architecture as a youth. He proved
even more restless than Wright and left M.I.T. after a
year. The education the school offered him, he said,
was "architectural theology," designed to teach him
the *history* of past architecture. To his way of thinking,
it offered nothing in the way of training in the *theory* of
beautiful, harmonious design. After a brief stint in
Paris at the Ecole des Beaux-Arts, then considered the
finest school of architecture in the western world,
Sullivan had become disenchanted again and had
headed for Chicago.

He was soon one of the major contributors to the new Chicago School, and in 1881 he became Adler's partner. Sullivan's unique contributions to the firm were unquestionably his creative ability and his ability to formulate a theory of design that other, younger members of the firm could understand and take inspiration from.

It was Sullivan, for example, who declared that in the finest architecture, "form follows function." Sullivan meant that the architecture of any structure should grow organically, in other words naturally, out of such considerations as its function in society.

To put the idea in simpler terms, he believed that a building that was meant to be a railway terminal ought in some way to express the ideas of movement, of industrial might; it should not try to disguise its true purpose behind a facade that looked like part of a Roman temple. In the same way, he found it ridiculous to build New England style houses, with steep roofs meant to shed snow and small windows meant to hold in the heat, in climates that were hot year round. He noted that America was fast becoming a major industrial nation, and he thought architects should get to know the new materials and the new technologies and find a way to use them architecturally. Any material, any method, he thought, when it is used properly, can look beautiful.

While Wright developed no special relationship with Adler, he instantly became Sullivan's favorite among the young apprentices and soon was made the older man's chief assistant and draftsman. Indeed, Frank gladly became "a good pencil in the Master's hand," perhaps the last time he would ever allow himself to follow another man's lead.

The two became friends, as well, for they shared many qualities in common. Both were small and muscular, both liked music, both were accomplished artists, bookish, and given to thinking deeply about their work. Both were fascinated by nature and took deep pleasure in studying the structures of living things—for example, the way a tree grew and supported itself, the colors of stone and earth, the patterns of moving water, the grain of different woods. Both believed that the architect was, among all artists, the one most capable of satisfying society's social and spiritual needs through his or her influence on the man-made environment.

Despite his mentor's difficult personality, Wright professed reverence for the gloomy, brilliant Sullivan, nicknaming him "Liebermeister," or Beloved Master. In fact, Wright would soon model many aspects of his personal style on Sullivan, and would continue to do so throughout his life. Wright's florid dress, dazzling sketching technique, self-complimentary manner of speaking, easy arrogance—all reflected the affect on the impressionable young man of the charismatic Sullivan. Wright picked up the affected third person mannerism when referring to himself from Sullivan.

Wright's true training as a working architect can accurately be said to have taken place during the years of his employment at Adler & Sullivan. Neither partner had an interest or particular talent for designing private homes. Periodically a request to design a house would come in from one of the firm's many business clients, and rather than turn such business away, the partners routinely handed off the requests to the firm's talented chief draftsman. Wright jumped at the chance. He had already given a great deal of thought to how he might improve on house design, specifically the design of houses built upon the flat landscape of the Midwest, and he was more than ready to put thoughts into action.

Writing some years later in *The Natural House*, Wright would describe what the current state of housing was in his view: "essentially, whether of brick or wood or stone, the Midwestern 'house' was a bedeviled box with a fussy lid; a complex box that had to be cut up by all kinds of holes made in it to let in light and air, with an especially ugly hole to go in and out of. The holes were all 'trimmed'; the doors and the windows themselves trimmed; the roofs trimmed; the walls trimmed. Architecture seemed to consist in what was done to these holes." He thought most of the trimming no better than empty gestures whose original purposes, if there had been any, were long since forgotten.

Meanwhile, Wright was becoming tired of being a solitary bachelor. All these thoughts about what a house and home ought to be made him wish to start a family of his own. By 1889 his future in the architectural profession seemed sufficiently secure that he could turn his attention to finding a wife. He took little time to settle on Catherine Tobin, daughter of a successful Chicago businessman. They were married that same year. As part of settling down, he asked for and received from his employers a five-year contract, one that made him the highest-paid draftsman in Chicago and guaranteed him some security.

Wright also persuaded his firm to lend him enough money to buy a building lot in the Chicago suburb of Oak Park, a favored bedroom community of up-and-coming Chicago businessmen. His mother, forever reluctant to let him out of her sight, persuaded him to renovate an already-existing small house on the property, and she moved in with Frank's two unmarried sisters. With more borrowed money, Wright designed and built a second house next door for himself and his bride. A modified shingle-style cottage of six rooms, it was more traditional than his oft-heard criticisms of American houses would lead one to expect of the young individualist, but then he was still only twenty-two years old.

To add to his income, and probably to give him more opportunities to experiment, Wright began taking private commissions at home at night and on weekends—what he described as his "boot-legged houses." Two of these houses are interesting to examine because they seem to represent evolutionary steps in Wright's artistic growth. One is the James Charnley townhouse on Astor Street in Chicago, designed in 1891. Though Wright was entirely responsible for its design, it shows the influence of Louis Sullivan in its elaborate decorative details. Yet the house for Dr. Allison Harlan, also in Chicago and designed the same year, is genuinely innovative and perhaps the first structure deserving of being called the work of Frank Lloyd Wright himself. The Harlan house design was the first time that the idea of inner space—the space inside the house—was more important than the physical structure of the house—the walls, the roof, and so on. This also eventually led him to the idea that the inside of a dwelling should be in harmony with the outside surroundings.

A year and a half later, Sullivan found out that Wright was secretly doing work for Harlan, one of Adler & Sullivan's clients. He became furious, wouldn't listen to any explanations, and summarily fired his young assistant. It would be many years before the two men would speak to one another again. "I went home, my shame doubled," Wright would later recall. "Although I often felt drawn to him in following years, I never went near him after that. It was nearly twenty years before I saw him again. The bad end to a glorious relationship has been a dark shadow to stay with me the days of my life."

Sullivan and his partner were soon to separate, too. Adler went off to work for a large elevator manufacturing company, and Sullivan, though he tried to continue in architecture on his own, found himself unable to keep a business afloat. Wright did eventually get in touch with Sullivan again, when the old man was in his final years and in a desperate state financially and creatively. To Wright's credit, he did his best to help his mentor, even when he himself hardly had a dollar to spare.

While Frank continued working mostly at home, he soon opened a part-time architectural office in the city, sharing space but not commissions with Cecil Corwin, another former Silsbee draftsman. Wright admired Corwin's easy sociability, and from the time they first met he was inclined to use his more polished associate as a model of how a professionally ambitious young man ought to dress and behave. Work began flowing Wright's way—remodeling jobs, additions, and then whole houses.

His first full-scale commission as an independent architect was a house for William H. Winslow, in River Forest, Illinois, in 1894. While the design for the house followed then-current architectural conventions such as post-and-beam construction, it had a number of features that suggested the direction in which Wright's imagination was going. Chief among these features were the broad, overhanging eaves of the roof, the earth tones of the building materials, and the manner in which Wright designed the ground floor of the house to emphasize its rootedness with the ground on which it stood.

This house and subsequent ones of his design, built mostly in and around Oak Park, soon drew the attention of the most influential architect in Chicago, Daniel Burnham. Burnham approached Frank and offered to pay for several years of training for him in Europe, still considered the source of the finest artistic education, on the condition that the young architect would join Burnham's firm afterward as a design partner.

In the interview that took place between the two men, Burnham told Wright that he could see "all America constructed . . . in noble, dignified, classic style. . . . Sullivan and Richardson are well enough in their way, but their way won't prevail—architecture is going the other way." Though Wright was eager to make his way in the Chicago architectural community, and certainly recognized Burnham's invitation as a golden invitation to make his way to the top of his profession, he declined the offer. Even more important than the approval of his peers to Wright was his search for his own inner vision of an appropriate Midwestern architectural style, a style appropriate for the magnificent prairie lands that he knew and loved. He was certain that such a style could only be found at home, and in his own way.

As Wright had hoped, his private practice grew with remarkable speed in the first years. It wasn't only that he did good work; he was also careful to cultivate the appearance of respectability in suburban Oak Park, which was full of potential clients. Wright dined at the best restaurants, joined the right clubs, began speaking to civic organizations, wrote articles about architecture and city planning for the newspapers, and patronized the theater, concert halls, and museums, where he often met the right sort of people. He even kept fine horses and, when they became the mark of success, bought an expensive car. He dressed well, too, if a bit extravagantly. His wife, Catherine, did her part, holding social teas for the prominent members of Oak Park society, joining ladies' clubs, and managing a great deal of entertaining at home.

A group photograph of some of the Wright clan. Frank Lloyd Wright is at the far left.

Unfortunately, Wright was living beyond his means, a habit that would follow him throughout his life. Though he kept ten assistants on his payroll, he privately worried about money, and as his family grew, his financial concerns mounted. He was frequently as much as eight or nine months behind on some of his bills, and reportedly owed one of the grocery merchants in town $5,000 at one time. To make matters worse, the Wright household during those years was very chaotic and did not provide the best working environment.

Six children came along in quick succession—Lloyd, John, Catherine, David, Frances, and Llewellyn, and though he would add bedrooms, running them out here and there from the original central house, there never seemed to be enough space for all of them. The Wrights were attracted to what was then called "progressive" parenting, which meant that the children were often allowed to do pretty much as they pleased. Noisy, given to tearing up the well-furnished house in their high-spirited play, they made serious concentration on the work at hand very difficult sometimes. There were also many relatives living at the Oak Park address. In addition to Wright's often overprotective and temperamental mother, there were often members of Catherine's family on hand as well.

By all accounts, Wright did his best to ignore the chaos. Indeed, he seems to have had an ability to all but ignore his children. A telling illustration of how oblivious Wright could be was related years later by one of his assistants, Albert McArthur. Albert, a chronic jokester, one day grabbed a passing Wright child and shouted to the father, "Quick now, what's the name of this one?" Wright, flustered, gave the wrong name. Wright later confirmed that parenthood and architecture could not mix well in his life. Father-feeling, he said, was something he felt only for the buildings he designed. His children he regarded as "play-fellows" at best. His relationship with Catherine was reportedly no better.

If Wright paid little attention to his immediate family, he still remained close with his Lloyd Jones relatives. One of the more interesting works of these years was the windmill designed in 1896 for his beloved maiden aunts Nell and Jane Lloyd Jones at a progressive school they had founded in Hillside, Wisconsin. The windmill offered Wright an opportunity to have some fun architecturally and to try out some of the inventive imagination for which he would eventually become famous. He drew up plans for a windmill unlike any that had ever been seen in Wisconsin, where slender tripod-shaped iron and steel structures were the rule. He called his invention the "Romeo and Juliet Windmill."

The Romeo and Juliet Windmill, built for Wright's favorite aunts at their school in Hillside, Wisconsin.

The aunts, who were always among Frank's greatest supporters and who were quite used to his whimsical turn of mind, trusted his judgment and were ready to go ahead and build the innovative structure. It consisted of a sixty-foot high diamond-shaped tower (presumably Romeo), and a companion fifty-foot high octagonal buttress that hugged it (Juliet), all constructed of wood and shingles. But when they showed the windmill plans to the Lloyd Jones menfolk and to a local builder named Cramer, every one of them said the design was ridiculous. The men predicted it would blow down in the first strong wind.

Shaken, the gentle ladies telegraphed their nephew: CRAMER SAYS WINDMILL TOWER SURE TO FALL. ARE YOU SURE IT WILL STAND?, to which Wright quickly telegraphed back: BUILD IT. He followed the terse communique with a charmingly persuasive letter:

> Of course you had a hard time with Romeo and Juliet. But you know how troublesome they were centuries ago. The principle they represent still causes mischief in the world because it is so vital. Each is indispensable to the other . . . neither could stand without the other. Romeo, as you will see, will do all the work and Juliet cuddle alongside to support and exalt him. Romeo takes the side of the blast and Juliet will entertain the school children. Let's let it go at that. No symbol should be taken too far. As for the principle involved, it *is* a principle. I've never seen it in this form, but I've never seen anything to go against it, either.

Years later, Wright added this satisfied postscript to the windmill affair in his autobiography:

> Now nearly forty-four years have gone by since the amateur windmill tower—Romeo and Juliet—took its place on the hill in the sun overlooking the beloved valley. I, the author of its being, hair getting white now as Aunt Nell's was then. . . . Seemingly good as ever the wooden tower that was an experiment still stands in full view. Shall I take it down, faithful servant serving so long, so well? Or shall I let it go until it falls just as I myself must do—though neither tower nor I show any signs of doing so. . . . One never knows. But when we fall, there will surely still be those to say, "Well, there it is—down at last! We thought so!"

The Romeo and Juliet Windmill was followed by two dozen or more commissions in the last decade of the nineteenth century. On the face of it Wright had much to feel satisfied about in his career to date, and other architects in his same position might have settled back to enjoy themselves. But Wright was terribly restless. He knew he had not yet produced a building that fully expressed his architectural philosophy. Part of the problem as he saw it was that clients, who paid the bills and ultimately controlled what was built, needed to be better educated to what the new modern world had to offer.

In hopes of changing this situation, he took his case public at the turn of the century, writing the first of what would be many important speeches, articles, and books on the subject of architecture. In 1900 he delivered a speech entitled "The Architect" to the recently formed Architectural League of America, in which he told his audience that they had lost their way, becoming the servants of the business community, taking their ideas not from their own creative imaginations but from an uninformed and tasteless majority.

The following year he spoke of "The Art and Craft of the Machine" before members of what was then known as the "arts and crafts" movement, composed of artists dedicated to the preservation of hand craftsmanship and very much opposed to the machine. In this speech, Wright articulated a philosophy he had been developing for some time, that artists should stop clinging to the past and exploit technology (machines) as a new artistic tool. He told his unhappy audience that "in the machine lies the only future of art and craft." Wright made it clear that technology should not be used to falsify art—making mass-produced wood-carved sculptures, for instance—but should be used to create new art and new ways of seeing basic materials. Using wood as an example, Wright said the machine "by its wonderful cutting, shaping, smoothing, and repetitive capacity" could "emancipate" the true nature of wood, revealing the beauty of its grain and color. He urged his listeners not to fight what he saw as both good and inevitable but to join forces with the machine, master its principles and possibilities, and make its production more beautiful.

Wright was obviously not a man who could be counted on to tell people what they wanted to hear. He had a mind of his own, and he was sure enough of what he believed that he felt duty-bound to convince others.

The Larkin Building, one of Wright's first industrial works, was intended to give workers a more humane working environment.

CHAPTER 3

GOOD TIMES, BAD TIMES
1900-1909

In the first decade of the twentieth century, between his thirty-third and forty-third years, Wright produced many of the greatest houses of his lifetime. Numbering more than fifty commissions in all, most were built in and around Oak Park, Illinois, and most represented moments in the evolution of ideas that would come together in what was called the Prairie style.

Not unlike Sullivan, Wright believed that the form of a building should follow its function. But for the younger man, that meant "the destruction of the box"—the traditional rectangular room—as a way to contain and shelter people. In its place, Wright proposed a new kind of house, one that was more organic, more intimately connected to the earth. The house design should not be so much about walls and frame-work and surface ornament for their own sake as it should be about the flow of spaces and the penetration of light within.

Years later, Wright would discover to his dismay that the same notion had been proposed more than 2,000 years earlier by the Chinese philosopher Lao-tze, who had observed that the usefulness of a water pitcher was to be found in the emptiness where water might be put, not in the form of the pitcher or the material of which it was made.

As Wright often would explain later on, the walls, floors, roofs, windows, and doors were merely the raw materials of architecture. The quality of the space within and without were the measure of its greatness and its true reality, "beyond time and infinity."

The Prairie House that evolved out of this concept was distinguished by its celebration of nature and its primitive elements—earth, air, fire, and water—and by the way its structure was made to cling to the earth as though actually growing out of the surrounding land. As the Prairie Style evolved over the next few years, it came to have a number of distinguishing features. Perhaps the most easily recognized is the great sweep-ing, overhanging roof that seems at once to extend the interior spaces outward toward the horizon in all directions and invite the outdoors inward.

Wright also favored generous balconies and ter-races, often lined with planting boxes featuring native plants and flowers, another way in which the house and the surroundings were joined. Pools of water were still another kind of horizontal element, one that had the added bonus of reflecting the changing colors of the sky. And horizontal ribbons of windows, with minimal vertical supports between glass panels, opened the rooms to the landscape. Wherever pos-sible, he brought the windows around the corners of his structures so that there were few if any sharp vertical edges to interrupt the view. To do this, Wright had to abandon the traditional sash window that rises and falls on a framed track; his windows were either fixed in place or were some kind of casement window that hinged outward.

Wright's favorite floor plan, the cross, also differed from the traditional rectangle favored by most of his contemporaries. With this arrangement Wright could put the fireplace—typically built of massive stones—at the center of the house where it could become a kind of symbolic heart. And he could arrange all the most important interior spaces so that they had plenty of natural light, in most cases some degree of sunny southern exposure. Another advantage of this plan was that it allowed him to cluster all the principal structural supports and the utilities—plumbing, heating, electricity, and ventilation pipes—in the central core, a very practical solution.

Construction materials also showed Wright's eagerness to experiment with the new. Steel beams, for example, with their extraordinary strength, gave Wright the technical means to abandon post-and-lintel construction in favor of the cantilever as a means of supporting floors and walls. (The cantilever is a horizontal beam held at one end only, yet it has sufficient strength to support heavy elements on the other end. The branch of a tree is, in a sense, cantilevered, as is a diving board, and many of the more modern bridges, but Wright was an innovator in using it in architectural construction.) Wright also was the first to use concrete as part of visible house construction.

Interiors were similarly innovative, as he abolished rooms with their square or rectangular floor plans in favor of asymmetric spaces defined by movable or freestanding walls, doorless openings between areas, and skylights that brought natural light and glimpses

The 1938 Chicago World's Fair, where Wright was first introduced to Japanese architecture.

of the outdoors deep within the house. Of all aspects of Wright's thinking on residential housing, it is this flexibility, the freedom of movement that it allowed, that has influenced modern architecture the most.

As time passed, it became clear to Wright that the furnishings within the house also had to be an integral part of the "organism," so he designed built-in furniture, architectural lighting, stained glass windows, and even the fabrics, rugs, and accessories that were to fill the home. In his use of color he preferred soft and subtle earth tones of brown, green, and gray, the colors of the landscape, over the brighter primary colors.

In many ways the Prairie House concept was reminiscent of traditional Japanese architecture. Although Frank had in fact seen such designs at the Chicago World's Fair of 1893, and although he traveled on a pleasure trip to Japan in 1905, he denied having been directly influenced. Perhaps as he said, the similarities derived solely from common artistic impulses.

The Winslow House, mentioned earlier, was Frank's earliest experiment in the Prairie House style. Despite its success, Frank had few opportunities during the rest of the 1890s to explore the style's design possibilities, except on paper. Most clients continued to ask for more conventional houses, and Frank was in no position to turn away business, however frustrated he may have felt about the results.

The Hickox House, Kankakee, Illinois, in 1900 marked a notable return to many of the features found in the earlier Winslow House. This was followed in 1902 by the W.W. Willits house, a widely acclaimed design, described by a critic as "the first masterpiece among the Prairie houses."

A lifelong problem for Frank's architectural practice was his failure to keep the construction cost of his projects within the price estimates he gave clients at the beginning. Fascinating examples of the manner in which Wright dealt with clients when problems arose are recorded in the letters that flew back and forth between the architect and two Prairie House clients, the brothers Darwin and William Martin, between 1902 and 1904.

Darwin was a top executive with the Larkin Company, a large mail-order firm in Buffalo, New York, and William was the owner of the E-Z-Polish Company in Chicago. William was also one of Wright's neighbors in Oak Park, and it was through that connection that he came to know the architect and his work. Not only did William want a new house built in

Oak Park, but he knew that his brother, Darwin, in Buffalo also was interested in a new house, and that Darwin's employer, the Larkin Company, was planning to build larger headquarters. William approached Wright to talk tentatively about commissioning him for some work in October 1902. He was dazzled by the man, as his first letter to Darwin on the topic indicates.

Dear Dar:

I have . . . talked to, admired, one of nature's *noblemen*—Mr. Frank Lloyd Wright. . . . He says that the way labor and materials are now, that he would not care to try for anything in his line *under* $5000.00—but thinks a design that would please me could be made.

I told him of your lot. . . . He would be *pleased* indeed to build *your* house—and further he is *the man*, has had *large* experience in large office buildings with Adler & Sullivan, was educated as a civil engineer, was head man in A.&S., and stood next to Mr. S. He says it is strange that he is only known as a residence architect—when his best and largest experience was in large buildings . . . he is *pure gold*. . . .

Darwin accepted his brother's judgment of Wright (which was obviously based in part upon Wright's own exaggerated claims as to his experience) and brought the architect to the attention of his boss, John Larkin. Larkin must have told Darwin that his first choice was the firm of Adler & Sullivan and sent him to Chicago to make inquiries, because some months later Darwin wrote his boss that the firm was no longer in business. He added,

But in their palmy days, Mr. Wright was the right-hand man. . . . Mr. Sullivan's and Mr. Wright's offices (were situated) side by side. In these two rooms all their work was created, and during much of the time Mr. Sullivan was away because of poor health. . . . The $500,000 Wainwright Building and the Union Trust Building of St. Louis; the Schiller Theater and the Stock Exchange in Chicago; the Seattle and Pueblo Opera Houses, all Adler & Sullivan work, were, I inferred from Mr. Wright, largely his creations. He also had as much to do with the Auditorium as a young man, just past twenty, could be expected to have. . . .

Once again, Wright seems not to have hesitated in taking credit for a good deal more experience than he had, and on that basis, as well as on the evidence of their eyes, all three clients signed contracts with Wright.

Both brothers would find Wright's disorganized way of working extremely difficult to live with, and over the two years plus that their houses went from the drawing boards to construction, the tone of their separate relationships gradually heated up from warm to very, very hot. Indeed, on several occasions the parties came close to canceling the work altogether.

Early on, for example, William wrote Darwin about Wright in only a mildly concerned tone:

> If you discover any way in your dealings with him, whereby you are able to keep tabs on him, I would like to know how you do it.
>
> I called his office yesterday morning, and one of the draftsmen said that he had been working on the plans, and mailed them to you Thursday. . . . He said that when Mr. Wright returned from Buffalo, he threw the plans into one corner of the office . . . and said nothing about any alterations until Wednesday or Thursday, when he inquired if the plans had been altered, and, much to his surprise, he was told that nothing had been done, as nothing had been said about it by him. . . .
>
> Certainly, if Wright's plans appear to be "queer," his business methods are more so. Probably his loose methods are a mere indication of his genius—because if a man is a genius, he must be a little off in other respects (?). I have fully concluded that while I thoroughly appreciate his plans and ideas, I would not give two cents for this superintendence of a job. . . .

Wright's indifference to the "superintendence of a job" kept him in constant hot water, and constant correspondence, with clients. Several months after William's above plaintive letter, the architect sent Darwin a response. Instead of trying to soothe his upset client, Wright scolded him for his impatience!

> My dear D.D. Martin:
>
> Your plans you have by this time, no doubt. . . .
>
> If the making of plans were as simple and as quickly to be performed as you think I for one should be glad. . . .
>
> Do try and have faith that we will serve you as we best can, for we will so serve you, but drawings are not going to leave this office for your buildings until they are right and fit to use as nearly so as we can make them at least, even if you wander homeless for the rest of your mortal days. Write us your needs and rest assured that we will hasten to give you whatever you require but if you don't receive it next day don't assume neglect, default, or unnecessary delay. It takes some time to arrive at correct information.
>
> You fellows down there (in Buffalo) put a Chicagoan to shame with your get-there gait, but be persuaded that the best results in buildings don't come with that gait. . . .

Wright would not budge in the struggle to produce "the most perfect thing of its kind in the world—a domestic symphony, true, vital, comfortable. A real . . . translation of those hard, faithful years into a permanent record that will proclaim me to subsequent generations as a lover of the good! the true! the beautiful!"

By the time the two years or more of negotiations approached an end, the brothers were struggling mightily to keep some kind of control over costs and results. William felt compelled to warn his brother, "Be *very* careful in your dealings with him. If he is sane, he is *dangerous*."

Eventually, when the work was ended and the houses did in fact more than meet their owners' expectations, peace returned between them and the architect. Wright received a total of nine design commissions through the Martin brothers, and they became among his staunchest allies during the difficult years ahead.

The Larkin commission turned out to be one of the major creations of Wright's career. The dramatic five-story Larkin Company Administration Building, in Buffalo, New York, in 1904, was the first vertical construction Wright ever completed on his own, and it demonstrated that he could be just as original in commercial work as he was in residential work.

Not surprisingly, the ideas contained in the Larkin building had much in common with those expressed in his Prairie House residential designs. Wright thought of the workplace as a part-time home for people and the employer-executives as benevolent parents who watched over their worker-children. With this in mind he designed an interior space that he declared was "ideal for body and mind." It called for the several hundred clerical workers—the file clerks and secretaries—to work on the large main floor, and their managers to be situated on the balconies above. A recreational area, a restaurant, and a conservatory were among the bonus features included to make working conditions more pleasant and to bring work-ers and managers together under less formal, more democratic conditions.

Other innovations in the Larkin Building that were new to the American workplace were the first build-ing-wide air-conditioning system in the country, the first large use of plate glass, and the first use of cus-tom-designed, built-in metal furniture and file cabi-nets. Handsome stairwells at the four corners of the building were ideas that came out of Wright's concern for fire safety: the stairs themselves were designed in such a way that they stood away from the surrounding walls, allowing for the rapid exit of personnel in an emergency.

The Larkin Building was a smashing success. *The Architectural Review* described the work "as fine a piece of original and effective composition as one could expect to find."

After the Prairie House designs and the Larkin Building, Wright's other major work of this time was the startling Unity Temple for the Oak Park Unitarian Church, begun in 1905. The building committee may have toyed briefly with the idea of erecting a traditional sort of church building, but Wright had something quite different in mind. He said to them, "Why not erect a temple to man, appropriate to his uses as a meeting place, in which to study man himself for his God's sake? A modern meeting house and a good-time place." To this end he thought the church ought to consist of two massive cubes, the larger one for religious meetings of the 400-member congregation, the smaller one for community and social functions.

He also persuaded the building committee to let him use reinforced concrete as the principle building material, an idea that was truly revolutionary at the time. Though they had reservations about the idea—concrete was then considered a crude, raw material, inappropriate for fine buildings—he was able to win them over on the basis of economy. He promised to make the concrete beautiful through an ingenious technique that exposed the pebble in the concrete mix, which gave the concrete's surface an interesting nubbly texture. This, he said, would make it possible for them to build within their restrictive budget of $35,000 and still have an elegant interior.

The buildings Wright produced—Unity Temple and Unity House—were unlike any other church complex then in America. There is nothing soft or gentle about their appearance; they are formal and severe, both inside and out. It is said that many parishioners prayed for ivy to hide what was to them an ugly pebbled surface, and praised the Lord when it finally grew. But there were many who saw Unity's beauty from the outset.

A reporter for one of the local newspapers congratulated the architect for what he described as Unity's "indescribable beauty." He found that "the eye and the mind were rested and the soul uplifted" by what they saw in the finished work, which "has the magic of grandeur to . . . inspire the spirit of reverence and desire for larger service."

As the end of the first decade of the twentieth century approached, Wright's work had broadened to include apartment houses, commercial buildings, and recreation centers. Still, in terms of numbers, residences continued to be his most important work. Two of his more significant residential commissions in this period were the estate of the Avery Coonleys, located west of Chicago and done in 1908, and the Frederick Robie House, built in the heart of Chicago in 1909.

The Robie House turned out to be the finest example of Wright's mature Prairie style and kind of a finale to this phase of his career. There was both nobility and strength evident when the house was viewed from any direction. Because of Robie House's ship-like appearance—it was mostly long and narrow and ran parallel with the street, like an ocean liner at the dock—German-speaking Chicagoans referred to it as *Der Dampfer* ("the steamship"). But Wright had another explanation for the Robie House's long, narrow look. His houses were meant to "lie serene beneath a wonderful sweep of sky," rather than challenge the landscape or pull away from it.

The interiors of the Robie House were among his most beautiful. Everything—from the furniture and woodwork to the rugs, lamps, tableware, and wall

paint—were controlled by Wright. Certainly, it took a
special kind of client to surrender all his choices to the
mind and vision of one man—but that is what Wright
demanded, and it is usually what he got.

   With so much going his way professionally, it
might seem reasonable to expect that Wright would
have been a happy man as 1910 approached. But in
truth, matters were quite the opposite, for his private
life was becoming intolerable. A romantic relationship
had grown between Wright and Mamah Borthwick
Cheney, the wife of one of his clients. By every indica-
tion their feelings for one another, then and later, were
mutually deep and satisfying despite the turmoil the
relationship would create. Mamah was a cheerful and
highly intelligent woman of strong will, evidenced by
the fact that at a time when few women attained a
higher education, she earned a master's degree in
teaching from the University of Michigan.

   In 1908 Wright had asked Catherine for a divorce,
which she refused, or perhaps as he later claimed, she
asked him to wait a year on the theory that he would
change his mind and settle back into his family. By
this time Wright had a distant relationship with his
wife and children. Shortly after refusing Wright a
divorce, Catherine wrote to Mrs. Ashbee, a close friend
in England, "I know that peace will come out of all this
turmoil and distress." After reading this, the wise
Mrs. Ashbee made the following entry in her journal:
"There is something tender and loveable about Mrs.
Wright. . . . I feel in the background somewhere difficult places gone through—knocks against many stone
walls . . . and I am certain I hear too beginnings of a
different kind of sadness—a battling with what will be
an increasing gloom and nervousness . . . in her husband."

   During that period he became depressed. He came
to believe that the revolution in architecture, which he

had expected to lead by his example, had failed. He began to lose interest in his work and was, in fact, so distracted that when Henry Ford interviewed Wright regarding the design of "Fairlaine," his palatial residence in Dearborn, Michigan, the architect made such a poor impression that Ford took his business elsewhere.

Meanwhile, Wright's work was beginning to win more attention in Europe. In 1909 he received an offer from a prestigious Berlin publisher, Ernst Wasmuth, to publish a book of his architectural designs. Wright saw this as an opportunity to find a new audience—Germany was then the most progressive country in terms of its acceptance of modern architectural ideas. Perhaps he could regain his creative momentum with their help. He also hoped that by going overseas to supervise the planning and design of the book he could escape his problems at home.

Wright agreed to go at once. He put one of his assistants, Hermann von Holst, in charge of completing his works in progress, abruptly abandoned his wife and children, and left suddenly for Berlin. With him went Mrs. Cheney, who would later be known by her maiden name, Mamah Borthwick. In making this dramatic move, Wright had effectively withdrawn himself from the scene of American architecture; for how long, no one could say.

The newspapers across the country seized on these events in the controversial architect's life and made them front-page sensations. Crowds of reporters besieged the Wright home on Oak Park, clamoring for a statement from Catherine. With characteristic dignity, Catherine issued the following statement: "My heart is with him now. He will come back as soon as he can. . . ." While one can admire Catherine's loyalty, her skill in predicting the future would prove to be sadly flawed.

Wright (*left*) on one of his many trips to Japan, accompanied by his architectural assistant Antonin Raymond.

CHAPTER 4

TRIUMPH AND TRAGEDY
1910-1914

If 1909, the year of Wright's departure from America, marked a low point in his career, the following year certainly represented a much higher one. The double portfolio of his design sketches was prepared and published in 1910.

To avoid distraction while creating this portfolio, Wright went to Florence, Italy, leaving his friend Mamah behind in Germany. Working in a rented apartment, and assisted by one of his draftsmen and his son, Lloyd, the architect produced numerous beautiful drawings based on the sketches brought from the United States.

This was in several ways an idyllic period for Wright, but from time to time he reflected on his past actions. On one occasion he concluded that his behavior had been "selfish, cruel, a waste of life and purpose. . . . What a traitor I seem to the trust that has been placed in me by home, friends, and not the least the cause of Architecture." But it was not his nature to be self-critical for long, and he soon had something to be cheerful about.

The publication of the portfolio of his works brought him to the attention of European architects and critics. Almost instantly he received wide praise from those members of his profession who had been struggling, as Wright had, to break away from the styles and fashions that had ruled Old World architecture for so many centuries.

The words of Erich Mendelsohn, one of Germany's leading architects at the time, stand as an extraordinary tribute to Wright's vision. After seeing the Wright portfolio, Mendelsohn wrote, "Inexhaustible the richness of his form. . . . His creation stands at the center of our time. Where yet is his equal to be found?" J. J. Oud, equally prominent in the Netherlands, stated, "The figure of Frank Lloyd Wright towers so assuredly above the surrounding world that I make bold to call him the very greatest of our time without fearing that a later generation will have to reject the verdict." The portfolio was soon followed by another book, a photographic record of Wright's constructed work to date.

But Wright could not afford to stay abroad, enjoying the praise forever. While Mamah returned to her husband's home and began negotiating a divorce, Wright returned home to the furor of social disapproval in October 1910. When he arrived at the train station in Oak Park, he called his former client, William Martin, asking Martin to meet him and drive him home. Martin described the event in a letter to his brother, Darwin:

> . . .He arrived promptly. . . . Wright was dressed to closely resemble the man on the Quaker Oats package. . . . Knee

trousers, long stockings, broad-brimmed brown hat, cane, and his lordly strut. He shook hands and he proceeded to apologize for putting me to the trouble, and said he really forgot for the moment when he phoned me what his position was in Oak Park, and I said, "Well, what is your position?" "Well, you know . . . I am a social outcast and of course no one wants to be seen riding around with me. . . . I am here not as a prodigal son or a repentant sinner, but I am here to set up my fences again, not as they were—that perhaps will not be possible—but will do it the best I can. I admit I have done wrong, but I am not sorry for myself. I am only sorry for my family, my children, and my clients who must have had to swallow humble pie in large quantities for my misdoings. People have been saying undoubtedly, "I told you so." Well, I am sorry for them all and now all I ask of society is to let me work. If they will only do that, let me work and do one more grand work before I die, I shall be content.

Martin concluded his description with: "He is as winning in his ways as ever. . . ."

Wright's ever-patient wife, Catherine, seems to have imagined, at least at first, that her husband was home to stay, and she gave him a warm welcome. And as if to show that things were indeed back to normal, Wright reopened the office adjoining his house and set to work trying to rebuild his architectural practice. But he found himself shunned by townspeople and clients alike, all apparently agreed that the eccentric architect had gone too far in his independent ways.

Within a few weeks of his return Wright wrote to a friend, "I have finally kicked the props from under what tolerance the ordinary person ever had for me. . . ." He reported that women drew their skirts aside as they passed him on the street, and his old friends crossed the road to avoid speaking to him. Worse yet, his old clients were refusing to pay up outstanding accounts as a form of protest.

Anna Wright, concerned for her son's future, made him a gift of several hundred acres of land near their family's hometown of Spring Green, Wisconsin. She

The living room at Taliesin, Spring Green, Wisconsin. The house was a refuge for Wright and an incubator for his architectural ideas.

hoped that this would persuade him to leave Oak Park and his troubles. It worked. Wright began designing and building a new dwelling there for what he anticipated privately would be a fresh start in his restless life.

Called Taliesin, a Welsh term for "shining brow," the house marked a symbolic return for Wright, in that it brought Frank back to the land of his mother's people and to the rural landscape and way of life from which he had sprung. It also offered an escape from the disapproving eyes of the public and his professional peers, who were clustered around Chicago. In a sense, Taliesin's very design seemed to express Wright's feelings about how he would live in the future, for the L-shaped structure was built into the hillside like a medieval fortress. Its low eaves, deepset windows, encircling courtyards, and well-placed shrubbery made Taliesin both a commanding presence in the countryside and a secure retreat from outside curiosity seekers.

Taliesin was also designed to be self-sufficient—a place where many people might work in peace and comfort. In addition to living quarters for the owner, it had drafting rooms, a game room, farm buildings, stables, a granary to store feed for the animals, and its own power and water supply.

When the house was complete in 1911, Frank announced he was leaving Catherine and the children, closed the office in Oak Park, and moved his practice to Taliesin. He was soon joined there by Mamah Borthwick.

Wright fervently hoped that Spring Green would accept him as Oak Park had not, and as a gesture toward explaining himself to his neighbors and the public at large, he called a press conference on Christmas Day, 1911. He then read a statement to the assembled reporters, telling them that he had left home and family because he found it impossible to be a father and an architect simultaneously. Giving "expression to certain ideals in architecture" had become more urgent than fatherhood, he said. Since he was an artist, and since modern society had need of the vision of the future that he possessed, he had no choice but to answer that higher calling, whatever the personal cost.

He admitted having violated the rules of social conduct by leaving Catherine and taking up with Mamah, but he said those rules "are made for the average," which he certainly was not. "The ordinary man cannot live without rules to guide his conduct," Wright readily conceded, but he said that he should be given credit for having the courage to take a more risky course. "It is infinitely more difficult to live without rules but that is what a really honest, sincere, thinking man is compelled to do." He concluded his "Christmas Message" by insisting that since the artist contributed to the improvement of society, that others should allow him greater freedom in how he conducted his life.

The reporters were definitely not persuaded by his argument; indeed, some thought he was quite crazy. Headline stories appearing in the newspapers in the next few days scolded Wright and Mamah for abandoning their families, particularly on such a hallowed day as Christmas, and they ridiculed Wright's plea for tolerance. Wright felt obliged to answer the articles with more statements to the press a few days later, but he only made matters worse. He denounced the returning reporters as "boobs," then restated his argument in even bolder fashion. Needless to say, the "Christmas Message" destroyed any chance Wright had to settle quietly into the community life of Spring Green.

Not only was Wright's personal life debated in living rooms all over the country, but conservative Spring Green was very embarrassed by all the commotion. The local newspaper ran an editorial declaring Wright's behavior "an insult to decency" and suggesting that the architect, if he wasn't just plain insane, was engaging in a desperate publicity stunt, designed to bring even more attention upon himself than he already had with his "knee-panties, long hair, and other funny ways. . . ." The paper found the whole sorry matter particularly unforgivable because of the distinguished reputation Wright's relatives had earned in the area as crusaders against immorality.

Meanwhile, Wright's geographical distance from the center of business and industry—Spring Green was over 200 miles northwest of Chicago—was creating practical problems for the gathering of clients. Now, if a customer was interested in talking to the architect, it was necessary to make contact by letter, or worse yet, to travel several hours by train to Wisconsin to see him. Commissions over the next few years were few, and those were mostly from independent-minded clients who had come to admire Wright before his troubles and were willing to overlook his eccentric behavior.

One such job came from Avery Coonley, who wanted a playhouse added to his estate in Riverside, Illinois. Others were for the Angster house in Lake Bluff and for the adventurous Booth house in Glencoe, a suburb of Chicago, but they were hardly enough to pay Wright's bills. With a great deal of free time on his hands, the architect-philosopher turned to writing about his art and craft. In the process he was able to articulate many of the ideas that guided him in his work but which he had barely understood in his own mind before.

Particularly important to Wright at this time was a thirty-five-page book he produced called *The Japanese Print*, in which he summarized what he believed to be "the laws of the beautiful" as they applied to all the arts and to nature itself. Wright thought that a thing, whether it is a painting or a piece of furniture or a building, is beautiful to the extent that it captures the essential ideas of nature. And the Japanese print-makers, who were masters at simplification, had a special ability to give visual form to nature because they were not concerned with drawing things literally but rather as symbols of what they were inside.

When, for example, a Japanese artist set out to draw a pine tree, he was not trying to draw a particular pine tree but the *essence* or soul of a pine tree, and this he could do with a few brush strokes. Wright went on to say that architects, as artists, ought to follow the same principles, looking for the *essence* of *shelter* in the houses and buildings they designed.

More intrigued with Japanese design than ever, and with too little to do at home, Wright was thrilled when he received an invitation from Emperor Yoshihito of Japan to pay a visit in 1913. The emperor had in mind to construct a massive hotel in Tokyo, its purpose to serve as a social center for the foreign businessmen and visitors who were beginning to come to the island nation in large numbers. Yoshihito wisely reasoned that a Westerner might have a better sense of what Americans and Europeans wanted in the way of hotel comforts and conveniences than would a Japanese architect who came from a different culture. And since Wright was known to be both innovative and very sympathetic to the Japanese, he was the first to be considered for what would eventually become the world-famous Imperial Hotel.

Wright won the commission easily and stayed in Japan for several months to work out some of the preliminary details. While there, he had plenty of time to indulge in his passion for Japanese prints, acquiring numerous additional examples, some of which he intended to keep for his growing collection, the rest to sell to American collectors. Indeed, Wright soon turned his reputation as a knowledgeable collector into a secondary business as a dealer, so that throughout his career he bought and sold prints at considerable profit to himself. As one of his biographers has written, Wright used his Japanese prints the way many people use credit cards today, cashing them in when all other sources of income failed him.

Wright returned to Wisconsin and was preparing further sketches for the hotel project when he won what appeared to be an assignment that was to seal his reputation as one of America's finest architects. The commission, which came in late 1913, was from Edward Waller, Jr., the son of one of Frank's early clients. Wright was asked to do the designs for Midway Gardens, which was to be a lavish, block-long entertainment complex in downtown Chicago. Large as the project was, Waller also insisted that the drawings be ready within a few weeks and the building completed in less than a year, an extraordinary challenge by any measure.

Not one to be daunted by the seemingly impossible, Wright "shook the design out of his sleeve," as he said, in a few days. He created not only the structure itself but designs for interior and exterior murals, paintings, sculpture, lighting fixtures, and decorative windows and doors. And true to his promise, the complex was ready the following August. Completed at a cost of $350,000, Midway Gardens was a massive brick and concrete structure that was both playful in its appearance and wonderfully logical in the arrangement of its parts, which consisted of coordinated facilities for opera, for classical and popular music, for dancing, and for dining, "a synthesis of all the arts," as Wright described it.

Original as Midway Gardens was, it was only briefly successful. The problem was never attributed to Wright's plan but rather to bad luck. It opened its doors on the eve of World War I, when gay nightlife suddenly seemed unpatriotic to most Americans. When a beer brewery with a German name sought to take over the faltering playground and turn it into a less elegant sort of place, Midway's popularity only declined further. The establishment went into bankruptcy in 1916. When Prohibition made alcohol illegal, the Gardens closed forever. It was eventually demolished in 1923.

But long before that, while Wright was still overseeing Midway Garden's construction, something inconceivably horrible happened in his personal life that was to destroy any optimism Wright may have had about improving his work prospects.

By 1925, Wright was recognized as America's greatest living architect. Later in life, he dropped the "living" and just made it the "greatest."

CHAPTER 5

PUBLIC SUCCESS, PRIVATE FAILURE
1914-1929

"Thirty-six hours earlier I had left Taliesin leaving all living, friendly, and happy. Now the blow had fallen like a lightening stroke. In less time that it takes to write, . . . an ideal servant had turned madman, taken the lives of seven, and set the house in flames. In thirty minutes the house and all in it had burned to the stonework or to the ground. The living half of Taliesin was violently swept down and away in a madman's nightmare of flame and murder."

Thus, Wright described the scene of desolation that greeted him on August 14, 1914 when he returned on the late night train from Chicago.

As best the police and reporters were able to reconstruct events later, Julian Carlton, a cook and handyman at Taliesin, had gone berserk in the middle of the noon meal. He had apparently poured kerosene or gasoline all over the kitchen and the rug in the adjoining room, then set fire to them. When some of the occupants rushed to put out the flames, they found that all but one of the exits had been locked, and as Mamah, her two visiting children, and the rest of the staff ran for the last remaining exit they were met by the crazed cook. Hatchet in hand, Carlton proceeded to strike each one down until seven lay dead and a number of others were severely wounded.

It was Will Weston, Wright's foreman of many years, who was finally able to subdue Carlton. Wright continues, "He had come to grips with the madman, whose strength was superhuman, but slipped away from his grasp and blows. Bleeding from the encounter, he ran down the hill to the nearest neighbor . . . to give the alarm, made his way back immediately through the cornfields only to find the deadly work finished and the home ablaze. Hardly able to stand, he ran to where the fire hose was kept in a niche of the garden wall, past his young son lying there in the fountain basin—one of the seven dead—got the hose loose, staggered with it to the fire and with the playing hose stood against destruction until they led him away."

Wright went on to tally the terrible cost in human lives: "She [Mamah] for whom Taliesin had first taken form and her two children—gone. A talented apprentice, Emil Brodelle; the young son of William Weston . . . David Lindblom, a faithful workman; [and] Thomas Brunker. . . . The madman was finally discovered after a day or two hidden in the fire-pot of the steam boiler, down in the smoking ruins of the house. He had swallowed hydrochloric acid, a caustic, to kill himself. Still alive though nearly dead, he was taken to Dodgeville jail. Refusing meantime to utter a word, he died there."

Wright first learned about the Taliesin tragedy back in Chicago while he was having lunch with his son, John, at a restaurant in the partly finished Midway Gardens. A long-distance phone call from Spring Green told him only that there had been a bad fire. On the train ride home he read the grisly details in the night edition of the newspaper.

Emotionally shattered by the deaths and devastation, Wright personally saw to the burying of Mamah in the family burial ground. "All I had left to show for the struggle for freedom for five years past . . . had now been swept away," he reflected as he turned the spadefuls of earth upon her plain wooden casket. He shut himself away from friends and remaining family for many days, eating little or nothing, trying to get his mind adjusted to the terrible events. Then, showing the resilient nature that had made it possible for him to return from so many earlier disappointments and losses, he managed to pull himself together and set about rebuilding his fire-ravaged Spring Green home.

Taliesin II, he declared, would rise on the same site, built on an even grander scale than before. "There was to be no turning back," he wrote, "nor any stopping to mourn. What had been beautiful at Taliesin should live as a grateful memory creating the new, and, come who and whatever might to share Taliesin, they would be sure to help in that spirit. So I believed and resolved."

While the construction work proceeded, Wright met Miriam Noel, a wealthy, high-strung sculptor, whom he would later marry. Miriam , who provided a substantial amount of money for rebuilding Taliesin, joined the architect at Spring Green shockingly soon after Mamah's death. She was not at ease there, not because of the impropriety, but because she was more accustomed to the excitement of cities than to the quiet of the country. By all accounts, their relationship was stormy from the beginning and would soon prove to be a colossal obstacle to the concentrated pursuit of Wright's work.

Meanwhile, Wright also began design work on the Imperial Hotel, for which his fee was to be between three and four hundred thousand dollars, a huge sum at the time. However, then as always, money meant less to him than did his professional reputation, and he brooded about the fact that the American architectural community continued to ignore his unique creative genius. He deeply resented the way in which architectural writers persisted in describing him as "one of a number" of protegees of Louis Sullivan, and of his Prairie Style as being based on Sullivan's thinking. The Prairie Style was his and his alone. His sense of indignation was raised further by what he perceived as the theft by younger architects of his design ideas, which often turned up as poor imitations in their work.

To set matters straight, at least as he saw them, he wrote a harsh letter to *The Architectural Record*, the most influential magazine of American architecture in those years. In the letter he made his case for the originality of his architectural ideas. He began by tracing his association with Sullivan:

> "At the expiration of a six-year apprenticeship, during which time Louis Sullivan was my master and inspiration, . . . I entered a field he had not, in any new spirit, touched, the field of domestic architecture, and began to break ground and make the forms I needed, alone, absolutely alone. These forms were the result of a conscientious study of materials and of the machine which is the real tool, whether we like it or not . . . which at that time had received no such artistic consideration from artist to architect.
>
> That my work now has individuality, the strength to stand by itself, honors Mr. Sullivan the more. The principles, however, underlying the fundamental ideal of an organic

architecture, common to his work and mine, are common to all work that ever rang true in the architecture of the world.

Wright then launched an all-out attack on his competitors, whom he dismissed as "boys" who willfully stole his ideas for lack of originality on their own part.

He charged that such a person was nothing better than a parasite. As would so often be the case in his public declarations, Wright's lush language greatly, if not almost totally, overstated the case for the existence of a wide conspiracy to pirate his design ideas. To the contrary, over the first decade of the twentieth century the exciting and distinctive quality of his design thinking had inevitably influenced architectural thinking in this country, though most of those who emulated his designs did so not willfully but unconsciously.

Many architects in the Midwest who knew Frank Lloyd Wright's work firsthand and recognized its value, had consistently expressed appreciation for his creative leadership. But after being subjected to his tirade, few Chicago architects were likely to continue to do so. Once again, Wright seems to have intentionally widened the rift between himself and the rest of American society. But he made the harsh attack as he was preparing to go abroad, this time for several years, so perhaps he just didn't care how he was viewed at home.

During the period from 1916 to 1922, Wright, accompanied by Miriam, made five extended trips to Japan to complete the designs and supervise the construction of the Imperial Hotel. The Imperial was to be one of his most intriguing and successful commissions ever, and Wright hoped that when it was completed it would also be a wonderful showcase to attract other foreign work on a similarly grand scale.

Perhaps the most challenging part of Wright's assignment was to design a multi-story building atop ground that was regularly shaken by earthquakes.

In his autobiography Wright described the engineering logic of the foundation's design and why it was able to deal with the temblors, or shock waves, of Japan's earthquakes. Deep foundations that have long pilings move back and forth rocking the foundation of a building. Wright reasoned that because of this "the foundations should be short or shallow," thus allowing the building to move with the motion not against it. The sixty or so feet of mud below the surface of the soil was also, as Wright put it, "a merciful provision—a good cushion to relieve the terrible shocks."

When the Imperial came through one of Tokyo's worst earthquakes in 1923 with only minor damage while scores of other conventionally built buildings collapsed or were bent beyond saving, the flexible design of the hotel's foundation was singled out for praise and wonder. Wright's Japanese associate, architect Arata Endo, wrote him in America to tell what happened on the terrible day. "What a glory it is to see the Imperial standing amidst the ashes of the whole city!" Endo explained that he had run to the hotel when he felt the first rumblings, grabbed a post in the lobby to steady himself as conditions became more severe, and watched in astonishment as the building stood firm.

Wright's foundation later developed some unique problems of its own, when the hotel footings, or posts on which the building stood, subsided in some places by as much as four feet in the soft mud. Major rebuilding of the understructure was needed then, but the basic soundness and originality of the idea remained intact.

Also praised, and justly so, was the idea of the pool, which proved to be of great value during the earthquake when firemen used its water to fight blazes in buildings surrounding the hotel. (All-consuming fire storms are a frequent companion of earthquakes.)

The Imperial Hotel in Japan, one of Wright's major commissioned works, remained in use until 1967.

On its completion, the Imperial Hotel was acclaimed internationally as an architectural triumph and one of Wright's major works. It remained in use until 1967, when the cost of renovating it to serve the changing needs of downtown Tokyo proved prohibitive.

During the period of the Imperial Hotel's construction, Wright also took on a complex of houses, studios, and gardens for the wealthy oil-heiress Aline Barnsdall. Built on her Los Angeles estate called Olive

Hill, the structures were done in a style that suggested Mayan architecture, with stucco walls, dramatic temple-like pitched roofs, and an enclosed central courtyard.

Wright was perhaps the only architect in these years who was interested in and informed about Native American building traditions, which like Japanese architecture, were based upon symbolic images and ideas. For example, Wright took the fireplace and made it the focal point of the homes he built. The hearth, like the heart in a living thing, was where the life of the family dwelt. A harmonious relationship between nature and the home was also reflected throughout his designs. As in Japanese architecture, the inside and the outside of the dwelling had to flow together. Everything from the materials he used to the shape of the roof had to be in keeping with nature. For instance, the horizontal line of his roof design was intended to shelter the house. It was "the line of domesticity," of comfort and security.

Since the Imperial Hotel was an all-consuming task, Wright was unable to give the Barnsdall job the attention it deserved. The client, who had her own strong ideas about architecture and wanted more of Wright's attention, was frequently unhappy with him. The two came close to lawsuits several times but finally reached a friendly truce in 1926 when the last stages of the work was finished. The Barnsdall House was eventually nominated by the American Institute of Architects as an outstanding contribution to American culture and is preserved today as part of the Los Angeles Municipal Art Museum.

While Japanese architecture and the Japanese instinct for harmonizing man's creations with nature gave new energy to Wright's creative genius, the intellectual demands and isolation of the long Tokyo job took a lot out of him. Miriam was becoming increasingly nervous and depressed, leading her at one point to leave their Tokyo apartment and retreat to a distant mountain inn. Wright feared that she was sinking into a serious mental illness, and in time this would prove to be true.

In a letter begging her to return to him, Wright reveals what is, for him, an extraordinary degree of humility:

> . . .You are quite right: I have no true personal culture. My talent has come between me and the things that bring [culture], usually by personal sacrifice. Instead of making the sacrifices myself I have been taking them from others as my *right*. And I see how it has hardened and roughened the points of contact—how I even handle my (Japanese) prints as though they are waste paper—and have hardly patience enough to hear a voice, any voice, besides my own . . . . Pride in my work has served to give me the self-respect that enabled me to *keep on* where it were best that I should fail—for my own soul's good. . . . What lives in my heart today and brings the groan to my lips at night, the sweat to my face, is what I have done to others—"Conscience-stricken," you say, and I am.

The letter succeeded in its purpose and Miriam returned to Tokyo. Finally, in October 1922, once again with the emotionally troubled Miriam at his side, Wright left Japan for the last time. Back at Taliesin, he won several new residential commissions in California on the basis of the Barnsdall project. Each of these new projects used a notable new invention of his, which would come to be known as "textile blocks" because of the way they were "woven" together structurally.

The hollow concrete blocks were made from a mixture of one part cement to three parts coarse sand. The damp mixture was packed into molds by hand and baked until hard. The resulting building blocks, some plain and some patterned with geometric designs on the exposed sides, were then used to build walls. Steel

The Barnsdall House (Hollywood, California, 1920) was based on Mayan architecture and fit perfectly into the hot, dry Southern California environment.

reinforcing rods were threaded through the holes in each block. Then concrete was poured into the hollow spaces from above. The finished walls were not only solid and strong but they were wonderfully heat-resistant in the hot Southern California climate. They could also be manufactured at relatively low cost elsewhere and delivered to the site ready to be put into place.

Wright had begun to think about this technique as early as his work on Unity Temple when he wrote, "Concrete is a plastic material. I saw a kind of weaving coming out of it. Why not weave a kind of building? Then I saw the sea shell. Shells with steel inlaid in them . . . . Lightness and strength! Steel, the spider spinning a web within the cheap, plastic material." What Wright meant perhaps was that he saw concrete as a material that could be formed easily (its "plastic" quality) and that could be made strong with webs of steel running through each block. Concrete when it hardens shatters easily under pressure. The web of steel rods would prevent this, thus preventing a building from falling down under pressure, say from an earthquake. This technique, which is called "reinforced concrete," revolutionized the construction of buildings, which could now incorporate many different shapes and textures as well as strength.

His favorite of these so-called textile-block commissions was La Miniatura, a small, exquisitely beautiful house that he designed for Mrs. George Madison Millard, a widow, in Pasadena, California. As was repeatedly the case in his building projects, the design phase was all excitement and pleasure, the construction phase a nightmare of roof leaks, disagreements, and overspending. But in the end, the Millard House was a triumphant design success, both for its happy owner and for the honors it earned in the annals of world architecture. Wright once commented on his artistic satisfaction with the building:

> "La Miniatura" stands in Pasadena against blue sky between the loving eucalyptus companions, and in spite of all friction, waste, and slip is triumphant as Idea. . . . Alice Millard . . . says she would have no other she has ever seen. She fought for it and finally won—whoever may think she lost. It is her home in more than an ordinary sense. It is the reward anyone has a right to enjoy in any sincere high adventure in building. . . . I would rather have built this little house than St. Peter's in Rome.

Wright even put six thousand dollars of his own money into the house to make its completion possible after a thieving contractor stole building materials. This job was followed by the Storer, Ennis, and Freeman houses, all in the Los Angeles area. Wright's son Lloyd served as on-site "clerk-of-the-works" at the Los Angeles projects. Although it seems most of Wright's children managed to avoid spending prolonged periods of time with their father, Lloyd, who had joined his father's profession, had become painfully wrapped up in Wright's business affairs. As clerk-of-the-works, Lloyd's task was to see that the architect's work was carried out to specification. In reality, this meant that Lloyd had to act as mediator between the arrogant architect, his father, and disgruntled contractors and clients. This would have been an uncomfortable position for anyone, but it was excruciating for Lloyd, who already felt inferior to his father and who was constantly subjected to his sarcasm.

The senior Wright, supervising by mail from Taliesin in Wisconsin, often treated Lloyd badly. He left his son to solve problems that really required his own attention, and Lloyd repeatedly asked to be relieved of his responsibilities. But somehow, the work eventually was finished, the clients satisfied, and the resulting work deemed successful by all concerned.

During the construction processes, Wright's spirits ranged from joy to gloom and back to joy again, so much so that all the people around him must have suffered. Writing to the Ennises, for example, he said excitedly of their house under construction, "You see, the final result is going to stand on that hill a hundred years or more. Long after we are all gone, it will be pointed out as the Ennis house and pilgrimages will be made to it by lovers of the beautiful." But then, writing to son Lloyd following a quarrel between them about the Storer house:

> I've just come from the Storer house. It's a tragedy from my standpoint, but I can see how hard you've worked to pull it out and I approve of many things you did. I have been thinking things over and I guess in the heat and shame of the failure and loss I've been thinking more of myself than of you, more heedless than I ought to be. You've got to stay here and the thing ought to be fixed up for you as well as may be. I took that stand with Storer, who broke out bitterly against you.
>
> And I shall be so with Ennis and Freeman. I think we should not try to work together any more but that needn't prevent

getting this awful mess into a fair shape for you as can be done by your cooperation. I shall forget your break with me and if in this spirit you wish to see the matter to a conclusion I am with you. If not, I'll do the best I can along these same lines anyway.

I guess you've had enough.

At the same time he was working on the California houses, Wright was also engrossed with the problem of how to create some kind of low-cost housing that could be made available to the ordinary citizen. In this concern, Wright was giving witness to his feelings that the architect had a moral responsibility to address social problems and give shape to the human environment through his work.

To this purpose he devised what he called "The American System Ready-Cut" building scheme. His idea was to use modular, factory-prepared components of wood and plaster, combining them in various ways to produce small and medium-sized houses. The procedure was not unlike that which Henry Ford was using in the assembling of automobiles.

Several private residences and apartment buildings were built subsequently using the system. But Wright was essentially ahead of his time in promoting modular housing, and the idea did not really catch on. His original sponsors backed away before he had a chance to fully explore its possibilities. In future years, Wright would return to the low-cost housing ideal several times, with the same frustrating results each time.

Meanwhile, he continued to have personal problems. In November 1922, Catherine Wright finally granted him a divorce, and the following November the fifty-five-year-old architect married Miriam Noel, despite her emotional instability. Wright believed Miriam was schizophrenic. "All would go happily for some days," he wrote in his autobiography. "The strange perversion of all that. No visible cause. . . . The mystifying reactions became more violent until something like a terrible struggle between two natures in her would seem to be going on within her all the time and be tearing her to pieces. Then peace again for some time and a charming life."

Many of Wright's biographers have wondered why he entered into this unlikely marriage, given how stormy their relationship had been over the years. In the biography, *Many Masks: A Life of Frank Lloyd Wright*, author Brendan Gill speculates that Wright felt an overwhelming sense of vulnerability at this moment in his life. His elderly mother, Anna Wright, had died at Taliesin a few months earlier. Though Frank had long struggled to gain some freedom from her control, she had nonetheless been an anchor of stability in his otherwise difficult life, and he may have felt the need to replace her.

The marriage to Miriam soon failed for a number of reasons. It is more than likely that Miriam's mental illness together with both of their artistic temperaments put too severe a strain on the couple's relationship. Five months after the wedding, Miriam moved to Los Angeles, where she continued to harass Wright with threatening letters and lawsuits. Never one to allow marriage to interfere with a love affair, Wright a few months later became involved with one of his former students, Olgivanna Hinzenberg. Within weeks of their meeting, he moved to ensconce her at Taliesin and gain a divorce from Miriam. Olgivanna was to be Wright's third wife and was to give birth to his seventh child, Iovanna.

If his architectural practice was not already suffering enough from these kinds of distractions, in the latter half of the 1920s Wright lost several large and important commissions. A huge ranch complex for Edward Doheny, a Wisconsin-born oil magnate, had to be abandoned in 1927 when Doheny was charged with bribing government officials to illegally obtain oil field leases. A summer colony planned for Lake Tahoe turned out to be something of a real estate scam and fizzled soon after Wright completed his drawings. Also cancelled were a thirty-two-story skyscraper for the National Life Insurance Company in Chicago, a planetarium outside of Baltimore, and a fantastic steel cathedral/skyscraper that was to stand over 160 stories high, several times taller than any building on earth at the time.

In some of these projects, most notably the Tahoe scheme, Wright was aiming to strike off in yet another design direction. Successful as the textile blocks had been, they were by definition, block-shaped. Nature offered no such rigid forms, he observed, and if he was to emulate nature, he needed a means of creating truly flexible, natural shapes, or what he called plastic, organic shapes. He also rejected the more traditional wooden posts and beams and the steel framing that had come to dominate modern European architecture. Ironically, though Wright had been a major force in freeing European architecture from its old patterns, they had chosen to seek a different kind of modernity in what they called the International style, which was severe, polished, industrial, and quite different from Wright's style.

In Wright's view, all styles but his were expressions of a straight-laced, autocratic, sterile, and unnatural society. As fascinated as he was with the sculptural possibilities of reinforced concrete, Wright now sought ways to enclose living spaces with what he called "folded-skin" construction, which was modeled on the form of the Native American teepee. He planned to use this new form first in the angular resort cabins at Lake Tahoe, which were never built, and later, in the San Marcos Water Gardens, in Chandler,

Arizona, which also failed to get beyond the drawings stage.

Wright tried to be philosophical about these disappointments, of which the Chandler project was the most bitter. He observed, "When a scheme develops beyond a normal pitch of excellence, the hand of fate strikes it down. The Japanese made a superstition of the circumstance. Purposefully they leave some imperfection somewhere to appease the jealously of the gods." According to Wright's thinking, his only mistake had been to make his work *too perfect*.

As the twenties rolled on Wright had little to be optimistic about. Approaching his sixtieth year, in what would ordinarily be an architect's most productive years, he had not had a notable success for a long time. He still lacked wide recognition in the United States, even the Europeans were turning their backs on him, his finances were in what amounted to near collapse, and he had neither a wife nor a particularly warm relationship with his grown children.

But Wright had discovered one part of his life that was satisfying—life at Taliesin—and he decided to formalize what had been a rather casual kind of meeting place for his followers into a real school. He would later recall, "Young people had come from all over the world attracted by Taliesin's fame abroad to share its spirit; to learn, I suppose, what message the indigenous United States had for Europe. . . . My life in the hills revived."

But before he had had a chance to revive his life, the bad luck that dogged Taliesin in the past showed itself again. Wright recorded in his *Autobiography*, "One evening at twilight as the lightning of an approaching storm was playing and the wind rising, I came down from the evening meal . . . to the court below to find smoke pouring from my bedroom. . . . Fire!"

Wright set up a bucket brigade to turn the fire back.

> I was on the smoking roofs, feet burned, lungs seared, hair and eyebrows gone, thunder rolling as the lightning flashed over the lurid scene. . . . Suddenly a tremendous pealing of rolling of thunder and the storm broke with a violent change of wind that rolled the great mass of flames up the valley. It recoiled upon itself once as the rain fell hissing into the roaring furnace. . . . In that terrible twenty minutes . . . Everything I had in the world, besides my work, was gone. . . .

All that survived were his Japanese prints, which were stored elsewhere.

Wright walked around the smoking ruins, pulling out bits of the precious Chinese porcelains, bronzes, and stone sculptures he had collected over a lifetime. He put them aside so that they could be woven into the masonry walls of the next Taliesin, rather like sacrificial offerings. "Already in my mind," he later wrote, was the resolve "to build better than before." And rebuild he did.

Demonstrating again his extraordinary ability to rise above adversity—and, for a person continuously in debt, his remarkable gift for getting people to work for him when the likelihood of prompt payment was small—with the help of Olgivanna, Wright rebuilt what would be called Taliesin III. To raise funds for the new construction, Wright was once again obliged to sell a number of Japanese prints. Even so Taliesin was threatened with foreclosure to satisfy an overdue $43,000 bank debt, which he somehow managed to forestall for a year.

Fortunately, in 1927 Wright was contacted by Albert McArthur, a former drafting assistant and now a successful architect in Phoenix, Arizona, about a collaborative project. McArthur wanted Wright's aid in building the Arizona Biltmore, a luxury hotel. It was McArthur's intention to use his old teacher's textile-block construction method, and he hired Wright as a consultant for a handsome fee. To forestall any possibility that Wright might be wrongly credited for the job when it was finished, McArthur asked Wright to declare in writing just who did what and Wright complied, publishing a letter to the architectural community in *The Architectural Record*:

> All I have done in connection with the building of the Arizona Biltmore, near Phoenix, I have done for Albert McArthur himself at his sole request, and for none other.
>
> Albert McArthur is the architect of that building—all attempts to take credit for that performance from him are gratuitous and beside the mark.
>
> But for him, Phoenix would have had nothing like the Biltmore, and it is my hope that he may be enabled to give Phoenix many more beautiful buildings as I believe him entirely capable of doing so.

The McArthur commission also led to Wright's meeting Dr. Alexander Chandler, an Arizona real-estate tycoon, that same year. Chandler engaged Wright to design a vast hotel complex called San Marcos-in-the-Desert near Chandler, Arizona. Wright anticipated that the project might finally bring him the recognition he deserved in the United States. While he waited for Chandler to advance him money, he persuaded one of his prosperous cousins, Richard Lloyd Jones of Tulsa, Oklahoma, to lend him enough money to move his staff to the site for a winter of planning and drawing.

When the needed help arrived, Wright dashed off the design for temporary housing—a wood and canvas encampment dubbed Ocatillo, after the spindly cactus growing there—and in the first weeks of 1929 he and fourteen others managed to get the tent-like buildings up and livable. Ocatillo consisted of more than twelve individual units joined together by a simple wooden wall that zigzagged back and forth along the ground and held the compound together. The wooden walls were painted a rosy color to imitate the late afternoon light in the desert. The angular canvas roofs were scarlet red, matching the color of the small red flowers of the cactus.

Describing Ocatillo later, Wright said its repetition of angular shapes—in the wooden walls, the roofs, the window openings, even the patterns on the rugs—recalled gigantic butterflies with scarlet wing spots, or the movement of rattlesnakes.

While his draftsmen-turned-carpenters worked to get Ocatillo finished, Wright concentrated on the hotel's design, which called for the textile-block system of construction and a most ingenious kind of layout designed to take full advantage of the extraordinary landscape. Wright conceived of the building as a series of flat mesas with gliding paths connecting its various parts. The design and the materials would blend perfectly with the Arizona desert landscape, with its severe horizons and jutting plateaus.

Wright married Olgivanna in 1928. She was, perhaps, the most stabilizing influence in his life.

Just when he thought himself within sight of getting Dr. Chandler's go-ahead to begin construction, the client abandoned the San Marco project. Instead of the $40,000 fee which was due the architect, he found himself with a deficit of $19,000 to add to his already mounting debts at Taliesin.

In February of 1928 Wright was forced to surrender title to Taliesin to his largest creditor, the Bank of Wisconsin. Most of what remained of Wright's art collection, personal effects, and farm implements were auctioned off. If all these troubles blunted Wright's spirits, one would not know it from his actions at the time. The following month the irrepressible architect married Olgivanna and left on an Arizona honeymoon in a luxurious Packard touring car, though he now had no place he could truly call home.

At this juncture, a group of Frank's wealthy friends and admirers formed a stockholding company named Wright, Incorporated, to rescue him and bring order to his messy financial affairs. These good samaritans included critic Alexander Wolcott, playwright Charles MacArthur, Wright's two sisters, and clients Mrs. Avery Coonley and Darwin Martin. The consortium purchased Taliesin, paid off Wright's debts, and set him up with a living allowance. They hoped in this way to shield him from his many debtors and—not too successfully—from his own personal extravagance. Wright's recklessness with money was, by now, well known to everyone, and nothing short of taking his finances out from under his control stood a chance of saving him.

Typical of the way Wright was likely to operate on his own was the story his son John told of the time when Wright was building Midway Gardens and his creditors had forced him to sell off some of his Japanese prints to keep them from seizing his assets. With the needed money in hand, Wright and his son set out one afternoon to settle his debts. To John's despair, here is what happened instead.

> A glance from the corner of my eye told me that an expansive mood was descending upon him. At Marshall Field's [a department store] he saw a chair that struck his fancy.
>
> "One hundred and twenty-five dollars," read the salesperson from the ticket that dangled from the arm.
>
> "I'll take a dozen, send them up to Taliesin." Next he ordered a dozen Chinese rugs. At Lyon and Healy's he saw a concert grand piano. He caressed its keys with his Beethoven-like fingers, then ordered three.
>
> Soon we were seated comfortably in the Pompeian Room of the Congress Hotel. The dinner Dad ordered was the envy of a gourmet who sat and stared at us. We ate slowly, luxuriously enjoying the music of the famous Pompeian orchestra. The inner man satisfied, Dad leaned back in his chair—the picture of serene contentment. It had been a perfect day, he had succeeded in plunging himself in debt again and everything was normal once more.

Wright, Incorporated, was at the very least a curious arrangement, with no precedent in the history of American architecture. But as his friends knew, Frank Lloyd Wright himself was a national treasure, and nothing less than an original solution was likely to keep him afloat and producing. In exchange for having his debts settled, Wright was expected to turn over a portion of his future earnings to his caretakers, assuming he was in fact able to secure commissions.

Then came the terrible stock market crash of 1929. Wright's prospects for getting any projects built ever again seemed dim indeed, and his stockholders settled in for what was sure to be, at best, a long wait on their investment. Wright, for his part, confidently told his friend Darwin Martin, "I have my best work yet ahead of me."

Concerned crowds gathered outside the New York Stock Exchange during the 1929 Wall Street Crash.

CHAPTER 6

YEARS OF REFLECTION
1929-1936

The Depression years were difficult for virtually all architects. The investment capital needed to finance large projects was simply not available anywhere except from federal and state governments, which were not about to put money into unconventional or experimental works. (For this reason, Wright was not included among the fifteen or so architects chosen to design buildings for the 1933 Chicago World's Fair.) Nonetheless, for Wright these years turned out to be useful, if not financially profitable, to his career.

To begin with, the architect seemed to regain control of his personal life, thanks in large part to the steadying influence of Olgivanna. With greater peace at home he was able to spend a substantial amount of time thinking about his architectural philosophy and what he wanted to accomplish in his remaining years. At an age when most people have long ago abandoned hopes of any unexpected grand upturn in their life, Wright looked forward with characteristic confidence to something wonderful happening. And in fact, many wonderful things did happen.

The change in Wright's personal life coincided with a change in attitude among America's architectural critics. At last the native-born prophet of modern architecture was beginning to gain listeners, if not paying clients, at home. Between 1929 and 1932, Wright published more than twenty speeches, articles, and essays at leading university presses and in major architectural publications.

The depression years were also the period in which he wrote his *Autobiography*, a brilliant if not always accurate statement of his life and purposes. Over and over again he criticized the conformity of American art and life, and he had harsh words for American cities, which he saw as becoming ever more uncomfortable and inefficient places to live. "Democracy needed something better," he said. He also published *The Disappearing City*, a proposal for an ideal city of the future, which got good reviews.

And his designs were shown in a remarkable exhibition at New York's new Museum of Modern Art. The show placed Wright in the company of renowned European architects like Le Corbusier of Switzerland and the Germans Mies van der Rohe and Walter Gropius. Perhaps even more importantly, the exhibit made it clear that while the Europeans were all proponents of what was known as the International style, Wright was unique in his vision and in his work.

The two major events in Wright's life in the early thirties were the establishment of the Taliesin Fellowship and the development of "Broadacre City," Wright's elaborate and idealistic proposal for a new kind of decentralized, more humane city.

The Taliesin Fellowship grew out of Wright's belief that America had failed to provide a good training ground for its young creative artists and craftspeople. He thought they could best learn by doing, rather than by studying abstract principles in books. He was also firmly convinced that creative people should not limit themselves during their apprenticeship to some single, chosen field of endeavor but rather should experiment in a broad-based kind of training. This to a large extent was the way he had trained originally, and it was the way in which he had tried to bring along a generation of young architects at his Oak Park Studio and at Taliesin. Now he hoped to formalize the method and to see it repeated in dozens of other "little experiment stations" around the country.

According to Wright's idea, students would apprentice themselves to master craftspeople in a variety of creative arts, including woodworking, glassmaking, pottery, textiles, landscaping, and a host of other industrial arts, becoming familiar with all the materials and the most modern technologies available. They would also study sculpture, painting, drama, rhythm, and dance. At the same time, students would contribute as community members to the upkeep of the farm, the buildings, the kitchen, or wherever they were needed, so that the center would be nearly self-sufficient. And the best of their products would be sold, not only to raise money for the center but to attract and win over an ever-growing audience for modern design and art.

To demonstrate his idea, Wright set about establishing his own "School of Allied Arts" half a mile away from Taliesin in the old Hillside Home School buildings he had designed back in 1901 for his beloved Lloyd Jones aunts in Spring Green. Wright's first group of apprentices, thirty young men and women, were accepted in October 1932. Paying Wright an annual tuition of $1,100, the students went to work almost immediately, spending part of their days in creative training, part in the hard labor of renovating and enlarging Hillside's buildings, and part in farm and kitchen labor.

Wright's Fellowship notion never spread beyond his own original group and, indeed, Taliesin was not always the peaceful, productive place the master had planned. Though Wright liked to compare his "family" to Robin Hood and his merry band, the architect and his wife tolerated no idiosyncracies nor independence of mind among the apprentices. Oddities of dress, beards, or any other form of "self-expression or self-indulgence" among Wright's followers were rigidly suppressed.

As the architect explained to a newspaper reporter on one occasion, the apprentices were expected to "be the fingers on the hands of Frank Lloyd Wright," carrying out his ideas and visions. They had to realize that any form of personal competition with their leader would get in the way of the master-apprentice relationship.

Among the many visions that the fellowship carried out at Wright's direction was the construction in scale model of a futuristic community called Broadacre City. Built as a 12-foot by 12-foot miniature and representing four square miles of urban planning, it contained many different kinds of structures that a city of the future might require. (Wright managed to recycle

many of his previously unbuilt projects in the Broadacre model, among them his planetarium, his steel
cathedral, two gas station modules, and several apartment houses.)

The essential idea of Broadacre City was rather
romantic. Wright envisioned a community in which
men and women lived peaceably, without racial, po-
litical, or economic conflict. Projecting his "city" to
occupy open space, rather than the confines that most
older cities had to contend with, he spread out his
houses and all other buildings on acre-sized lots.

He designed them with convenience, beauty, and
efficiency in mind. "Imagine," he wrote, "spacious
landscaped highways, grade crossings eliminated, 'by-
passing' living areas, devoid of the already archaic
telephone and telegraph poles and wires and free of
blaring billboards and obsolete construction. Imagine
these great highways, safe in width and grade, bright
with wayside flowers, cool with shade trees, joined at
intervals with fields from which safe noiseless trans-
port planes take off and land."

The largest buildings in Broadacre City were,
significantly, two vast school complexes. Also notable
as an idea was Wright's designation of the power
companies, industries, long-distance transportation,
and the like as government owned. The chief executive of Broadacre City was to be The Architect, the
individual in society whom he judged to be best
equipped to see that not only the buildings but their
occupants lived in harmony. Wright thought that in
his city of the future, there would be no place for crime
or social strife, no industrial pollution, and certainly
no crowding. Broadacre City was, in a sense, the
ultimate statement of what idealistic artists have
always hoped art could do for mankind, which is to
make life better.

Wright with his assistants Robert Mosher, Edgar Hoffman, and Robert Bishop (*left to right*) looking at the Broadacre City model at the Industrial Arts Exposition at Rockefeller Center.

If Wright's goals were clearly unreachable, he can at least be credited with motivating people to think about what was wrong with cities as they knew them in the 1930s.

The model was first shown at an exposition in Rockefeller Center, New York, in 1935, after which it toured the country. Thanks to Wright's natural gifts for publicity, the model proved an effective means of capturing the attention of the press. By now Wright no longer seemed quite so much the revolutionary as he had, perhaps because the times themselves were more liberal. Newspapers across the country took delight in publishing photographs of the handsome older man with his mane of white hair, his curious clothes, and his odd band of Taliesin Fellows, posed with their elaborate toy city. People who had never heard of Frank Lloyd Wright or even thought about architecture were suddenly interested in reading about his theories.

Despite what was odd, or impractical, in the life and efforts of the Taliesin Fellowship, its participants for the most part were very happy there, and the group prospered as a whole throughout the Depression. Wright was so pleased with the arrangement that he decided to establish a second Taliesin in Arizona. He had grown to love the desert landscape, and after a serious bout with pneumonia in 1937, Wright bought eight hundred acres of government land in the Paradise Valley near Phoenix. He decided that he and the school would divide their time, the whole group spending summers in the north and winters in the south.

Taliesin West, as the winter settlement came to be called, had its roots in the Arizona encampments of the twenties when Wright and his youthful staff had pitched their Ocatillo tent structures in the desert while working on the San Marcos resort project. As was always characteristic of the man, he designed his southwestern headquarters in a way that made the living and working spaces seem to grow out of the landscape, with the colors and texture of the building materials borrowed from the surrounding mountains. And as had been true of Taliesin in Wisconsin, the actual construction work on Taliesin West was largely managed by Wright and his followers, though by the time their labors began in earnest they no longer needed to invent work to keep themselves busy. As the Depression years came to an end and a new spirit of renovation and reform entered the country, Wright suddenly found himself busier than he had ever been.

The Johnson Wax Administrative Building was a result of the company president's enlightened view of his workers' welfare and Wright's genius for bringing these ideals into reality.

CHAPTER 7

THE GRAND FINALE
1937-1939

In the view of many people, persistence and unfaltering self-belief have a way of winning in the end. This philosophy certainly seemed to prove true repeatedly in the life of Frank Lloyd Wright.

As the U.S. economy picked up somewhat—or, perhaps more accurately, as Americans became accustomed to the Great Depression—Wright had several notable successes, including the Kaufmann and Jacobs houses and the Johnson Wax Building. Altogether, these projects summarize the three ongoing interests of the architect in his eighth decade: residential architecture on a grand scale, housing for the middle classes, and work spaces. These jobs finally established his reputation as the pre-eminent American architect of his time.

The first interest, residential architecture on a grand scale, had its beginnings in 1936, when Edgar J. Kaufmann, Sr., a wealthy department store owner from Pittsburgh, approached Wright to design a country house for his family. Kaufmann was acquainted with Wright as the result of his son, Edgar Jr., who had joined the Taliesin Fellowship two years earlier. Kaufmann had taken a liking to Wright, and he had been persuaded to underwrite the costs of Broadacre City.

Impressed with the results, Kaufmann invited the architect back East to Pittsburgh to design an office within the store. While Wright was visiting, the Kaufmanns took him out to Bear Run, Pennsylvania, where they owned a weekend cottage on a dramatic piece of property whose wooded terrain included a spectacular waterfall. The Kaufmanns walked Wright around the property, pointing out places where they thought a house might go nicely. They also took him down to the waterfalls and said that a lot of the family's time was spent on the great flat rock at the base of the falls. Mr. Kaufmann described it as a kind of focal point of activities, a place to have fun, to play in the splashing waters, to explore.

Wright apparently fell in love with the place immediately and when he got back home he wrote the owners, "the visit to the waterfall in the woods stays with me and a domicile has taken vague shape in my mind to the music of the stream." Wright asked them to send topographical maps, showing the precise rise and fall of the land around the falls, and Kaufmann eagerly complied, his curiosity much piqued.

To Kaufmann's dismay, he heard nothing for a long time, and when he could wait no longer he called

Frank Lloyd Wright

A PICTURE PORTFOLIO

Always a workaholic, Wright remained prolific even in his later years.

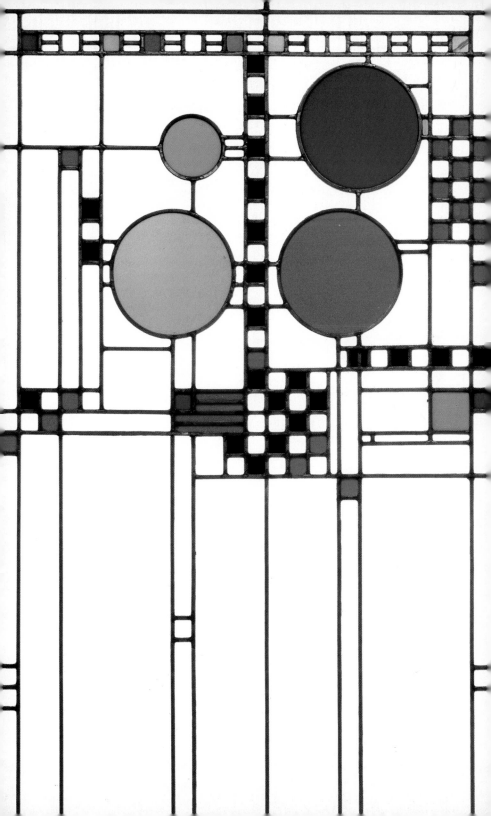

(Right)
The fellowship living room was the center of intellectual life at Taliesin West.

(Below)
Wright often designed the furniture for a building, believing that the accessories inside a dwelling were as important as the building itself. The simple, straight-forward lines of this chair are classic Wright design.

Fallingwater, the home of millionaire Edgar Kaufman, is perhaps Wright's ultimate statement on how the exterior of a house should merge with its natural surroundings.

(*Left*)
Wright worked in two, as well as three, dimensions, as shown in this textile design. This was produced by F. Schumacher as the Taliesin line of decorative fabrics and wallpaper.

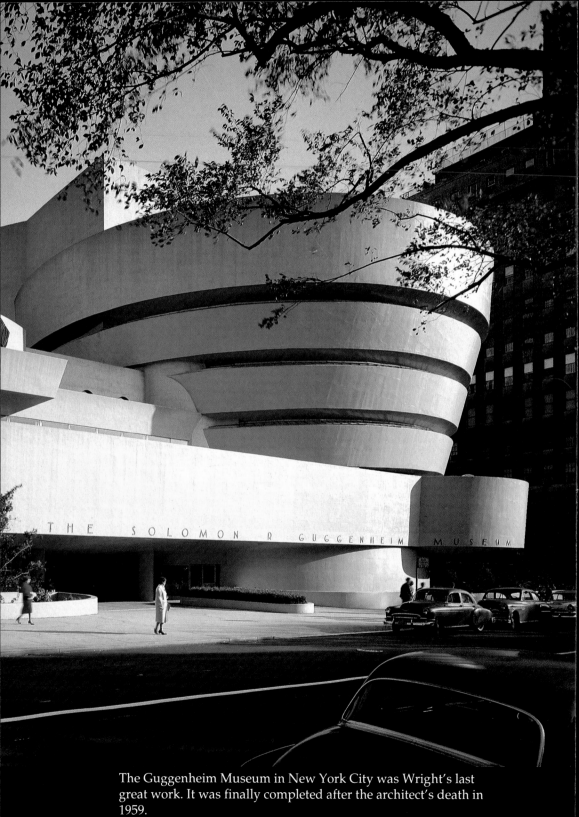

The Guggenheim Museum in New York City was Wright's last
great work. It was finally completed after the architect's death in
1959.

Taliesin, saying he was 140 miles away in Milwaukee, and wanted to drive up to Spring Green immediately to see the plans. Wright, who had shoved the project aside and forgotten about it, replied instantly and cheerily, "Come along, E. J., we're ready for you!"

Edgar Tafel, a Wright Fellow, remembered vividly what Wright did then:

> [He] hung up the phone, briskly emerged from his office, some twelve steps from the drafting room, sat down at the table set with the plot plan, and started to draw. First floor plan. Second floor. Section, elevation. Side sketches of details, talking *sotto voce* all the while. The design just poured out of him. "Lilliane [Mrs. Kaufmann] and E. J. will have tea on the balcony... they'll cross the bridge to walk into the woods. . . ." Pencils being used up as fast as we could sharpen them. . . . Flipping sheets back and forth. Then, the bold title across the bottom: Fallingwater. . . .
>
> Just before noon Mr. Kaufmann arrived. As he walked up the outside stone steps, he was greeted graciously by the master. They came straight to the drafting table. "E.J.," said Mr. Wright, "we've been waiting for you." The description of the house, its setting, philosophy, poured out. Poetry in form, color, line, texture, and materials, all for a greater glory: a reality to live in! Mr. Wright at his eloquent and romantic best—he had done it before and would often do it again. . . . Kaufmann nodded. . . .
>
> They went up to the hill garden dining room for lunch, and while they were away Bob Mosher and I drew up the other two elevations, naturally in Mr. Wright's style. When they came back, Mr. Wright continued describing the house, using the added elevations to reinforce his presentation. Second thoughts? The basic design never changed—pure all the way.

Edgar Kaufmann, Jr., later remembered his parents reaction to Wright's proposal. "I do not think [the waterfall site] had ever crossed my parents' minds. But once having been presented with the notion . . . it seemed perfectly good and proper." The siting of the

Kaufmann house, daringly cantilevered out over a waterfall in such a way that the horizontal levels of the house seem to be a natural extension of the horizontal rock ledges, is breathtakingly dramatic.

Even before its completion, it was celebrated internationally as an architectural triumph. One architectural historian has described Fallingwater as "the most famous modern house in the world"; another has called it "the best-known private home for someone not of royal blood in history." The thousands of visitors who continue to travel to its out-of-the-way location simply to see, enter, and enjoy this structure more than half a century after its construction attest to the accuracy of those descriptions.

The Kaufmann house contains characteristics of Wright's Prairie Houses of decades earlier, especially in its emphasis on horizontal forms and its daring use of cantilevered terraces of reinforced concrete, all of them seeming to grow naturally out of the hillside. But in Fallingwater he managed to bring all the parts together in more perfect harmony than he had ever achieved before.

Like so many of Wright's structures, Fallingwater's years of construction were difficult and sometimes marred by angry exchanges. The actual construction responsibilities were entrusted to a local builder, whose first efforts at working with reinforced concrete did not meet Wright's requirements and had to be torn down and redone. Matters between Wright and the builder became worse as the months passed, with Wright accusing him in his letters of a lack of ethics, a meddlesome attitude, mischievous interference, and general incompetence, all of which the poor man apparently took with good grace. Still later Wright fought with Kaufmann when the latter sent in his own engineers to check on Wright's progress and construction techniques.

Peter Wright (*left*), Frank Lloyd Wright (*center*), and Hib Johnson watch confidently as the engineers pile pig iron and sandbags on top of the pillar that was to be used in the Johnson Wax building.

The architect complained repeatedly to his client about the presence of Carl Thumm, Kaufmann's right-hand man, who watched over accounts and construction work on an almost daily basis. On one occasion he wrote Kaufmann, "I can't build this extraordinary house with a Thumb [sic]. . . . I must have my own fingers. I want to make a success of this house if I have a chance. A chance means very largely having my own way with my own work using my own fingers."

When the house was finished it had a number of minor problems—among them cracks, sags, and leaks. But this never bothered the owners, who adored the house. Edgar Kaufmann, Jr., later said of these flaws:

> Do these faults impugn Wright's ability? Fallingwater was an exploration beyond the limits of conventional practice. . . . Some of the great monuments of architecture have suffered structural trouble, precisely because they were striving beyond normal limitations. The dome of Hagia Sophia in Constantinople, the belfries of St. Peter's in Rome, the core of the Pantheon in Paris, all threatened the stabilities of their structures and require drastic repairs, yet these buildings still

stand and add glory to their countries and their art. My father was no monarch and his house was not conceived as a public monument, but Wright's genius justifies these references. No apologies are necessary for what he achieved at Fallingwater.

About the same time as his Fallingwater project, Wright was also giving considerable thought to a second issue of great concern, that of housing for the middle class. With this in mind he developed plans for what he called, with his usual flair for publicity, Usonian housing, the first two letters standing for "United States."

The basic premise behind a Usonian house was the creative use of inexpensive building materials, something he began working on twenty years earlier when he had tried to sell the idea of Ready-Cut modules. Then, it seemed, he was too far ahead of his time to gain attention, but now as the nation emerged from the Depression and there was a great need for additional housing, he decided to try again.

The Usonian idea first took tangible form in the Herbert Jacobs house in Madison, Wisconsin, completed in 1937. The Jacobs were people of modest income, and their budget, including the architect's commission, was $5000. Amazingly—given Wright's history of disastrous cost overruns—he delivered the house for just about that price.

The Jacobs house was made possible by a number of specific economies. For example, instead of a basement, which was expensive to dig and more expensive to construct, the Usonian house required only minimal foundation work, with a slab that "floated" on a bed of ashes and sand. Water pipes in the slab circulated hot water, and since heat rises, heat was radiated into the spaces above, eliminating heating ducts and radiators. The "ready-made" walls were of "sandwich" construction, with three layers of wood boards screwed together. The panels were sufficiently rigid to eliminate the need for conventional 2-inch by 4-inch stud framing, a labor intensive means of erecting walls. The slab roof design also cut costs in that it, too, was a sandwich of roofing, insulation, and ventilation ducts, replacing the more traditional attic plus roof.

Wright also introduced a number of innovations in the use of glass, in storage facilities, in spatial layout, and in furnishing that would make the Usonian house a forerunner of the modern American ranch house. If not as beautiful as Fallingwater, it was a realistic and remarkably attractive solution for moderate-cost housing in America in the 1930s, and it was hailed by many as such.

As a modern house for middle-income people, nothing like the Jacobs place had been seen before. People came, stared, then knocked on the door and asked the Jacobs' permission to come in and look around—so many of them that the Jacobs took to charging 25 cents, and later 50 cents admission.

Between 1936 and the United States' entry into World War II in 1941, scores of Usonian-design houses were built all over America. They included some of Wright's best work.

The third issue on Wright's agenda was designing more suitable work spaces for modern America. He got his chance, and then some, in a commission from the S. C. Johnson Wax Company in Racine, Wisconsin.

The architect-client relationship began in 1936 when Johnson's general manager, Jack Ramsey, was directed by the company's president, Herbert Johnson, to scout around for an architect to design a new headquarters building. Ramsey spoke first to a local architect named Matson, but when he showed some of Matson's sketches to Johnson, the director's daughter interceded, asking why her father didn't go talk to Frank Lloyd Wright. She had heard about him in school, and she was impressed with what she had seen and read. So Johnson dispatched Ramsey to have a preliminary talk with Wright at Taliesin. When Ramsey returned he wrote a report to his boss:

> Regarding the new building, I had a day Friday that . . . so inspired me as what can be done that I was on the point of sending you wild telegrams Friday night when I got home, or getting you out of bed on the telephone. . . .
>
> I haven't had such an inspiration from a person in years. And I won't feel satisfied about you getting what you want until you talk to him. . . .
>
> He's an artist and a little bit "different," of course, but aside from his wearing a Windsor tie, he was perfectly human and very easy to talk [with] and most interested in our problem and understood that we were not committing ourselves, but, gosh, he could tell us what we were after when we couldn't explain it ourselves.
>
> About Matson's sketch he was decent and honest. About the strongest remark he made was a bit of gentle sarcasm. . . .
>
> And he asked about what we thought this building would cost us. I said, when we got through with the building, landscape, furnishings, etc., we'd be investing around $300,000. He asked how many people it would house. I told him about 200. He snorted and said it was too much damn money for the job, and he could do a better functional job in more appropriate manner for a lot less. . . .
>
> He is very interesting to talk to, much interested . . . because it seems to hurt his artist conscience to see so much money spent on anything ordinary. . . . *Will you see him?*

Herbert Johnson did see Wright, at Taliesin, and the two men, both strong-minded individuals, disagreed about almost every matter discussed. As Johnson later reported the meeting, "He insulted me about everything, and I insulted him, but he did a better job. I showed him pictures of the old office, and he said it was awful. I came back from Spring Green and said, 'If that guy can talk like that he must have something.'"

The Johnson Wax Building is an exquisite example of Wright's efficient and aesthetic use of light and space in the work place.

Wright was equally excited with Johnson and the project before him. He had not had a large commercial job in more than ten years, and with Fallingwater soon to be completed he did not have any substantial commissions to look forward to at that moment. Wright described a second meeting with Ramsey and Johnson as a break in the dark clouds.

> They came . . . like messengers riding on white steeds trumpeting glad tidings. . . . Next day came a note from Hib [Herbert] enclosing a retainer [$10,000] testifying to his appreciation of what he saw. The pie thus opened, the birds began to sing again below the home at Taliesin; the dry grass on the hillside waxed green; the hollyhocks went gaily into second blooming . . . and the whole landscape seemed to have more color.

Wright knew at once the scheme he wanted to try—he had proposed it earlier on a project that had been dropped. Its most dramatic feature would be fifty-four concrete columns, shaped like golf tees, rising two stories from the spacious workroom floor to support the roof. Between the wide, circular tops of each column would be glass skylights, showering natural light down through the forest of columns. All the corners of the building would be gently rounded, as would the columns.

Not surprisingly, Wright's innovative columns soon caught the attention of the building inspectors, the government officials whose job it was to insure public safety in construction. Each column in Wright's architectural specifications was supposed to carry twelve tons of weight, but given the size of the columns the inspectors estimated that they would only bear five tons. When Wright refused to make the columns more massive, the inspectors called for a test on the site. A sample column was poured, was allowed to cure until hard, and then a crane was brought in to start loading pig iron and sandbags.

When the load reached twelve tons on top the inspectors were satisfied, but Wright, always the showman, ordered, "More!" Only when the load had reached sixty tons was Wright satisfied that he had proved his point. Work went ahead as specified.

The Johnson Administration Building was soon followed by the equally handsome and innovative Johnson Laboratory Tower, fifteen stories high with alternating square and circular floors cantilevered from a central service tower. By all accounts Wright succeeded in delivering his enlightened client the inspiring places to work that both had strived for. Wright noted with pleasure that as soon as the building was open, "streams of visitors from all over the world" came to see it. "Why? Because something universal is in the air. . . . High time to give our hungry American public something truly 'streamlined,' so swift, so sure of itself, and clear for its purpose. . . that ANYBODY could see the virtue of this thing called Modern."

This interior view of the Guggenheim Museum looks down upon the spiral ramp that takes viewers from floor to floor.

CHAPTER 8

END IN GLORY
1939-1959

Work now flowed in for all kinds of buildings. A commission came from Dr. Ludd Myrl Spivey, the president of Florida Southern College at Lakeland, to design an entirely new campus for the faltering Methodist institution. Needed were an administration building, library, faculty housing, industrial arts building, dorms, music building, seminar building, science building, art gallery, and workshops. Not since Thomas Jefferson had designed the basic buildings of the University of Virginia, more than 100 years earlier, had such an opportunity ever been offered a single architect. It would be Wright's only opportunity to carry out some of his ideas on city planning as well as architecture.

Wright designed eighteen innovative buildings, all of them using textile-block construction. Ten of these subsequently were built, with much of the labor done by Florida Southern College students. Particularly beautiful was the Pfeiffer Chapel.

With Wright's reputation for original work now widely recognized, official honors began to come his way. He was invited to lecture in the USSR and London, and later published these talks in a volume titled *An Organic Architecture*. He also made frequent speaking tours in the United States, where he took a certain perverse pleasure in prodding his listeners with outrageous statements. For example, he declared to an assembly of Los Angelinos that their buildings were "a dish of tripe"; he scolded Chicago real estate brokers for thinking only of profit; and he told a Milwaukee ladies group that they were more interested in their clothes than any ideas he could share with them.

When World War II began he even tangled publicly with the federal government. Determined to keep his apprentices from being drafted, he managed to get a number of people to sign a petition asking the government to set him up, in effect, as a one-man crucial wartime activity. The petition read:

> We, the undersigned, respectfully ask that the Administration of our Government authorize Frank Lloyd Wright to continue the search for Democratic FORM as the basis for a true capitalistic society now known as Broadacre City. We believe that work should immediately be declared a worthy national objective and the necessary ways and means freely granted him to make such plans, models, and drawings as will enable our citizens and other peoples to comprehend the basic ideas the plans, models and drawings represent and which, without political bias or influences will be invaluable to our people when peace is being considered.

Though this petition got nowhere, Wright was given a chance to take his case to President Franklin Delano

Roosevelt through the good offices of their mutual friend, Carlton Smith. In his autobiography, Smith told how the meeting went:

> So I took [Wright] to Washington and he wore a cloak over his shoulder and had a big cane and never took his hat off when he came into the Oval Room and he stopped at the door with great drama and said, so the president could hear, "You know, Carlton, I've always said I'd rather be Wright than President," and then he wheeled around and came up to the President's desk and shook hands with him and he said—and I will never know whether he thought this out in advance or whether it came naturally—he said, "Franklin," or "Frank," he called him, "Frank," he said, "you ought to get up out of that chair and look at what they're doing to your city here, miles and miles of Ionic and Corinthian columns!"

Considering that Roosevelt was paralyzed from the waist down and could never get up from his chair, this was a dreadfully tactless thing for Wright to say. It should surprise no one to learn that he did not get the presidential aid he sought.

With the war's end, and with Wright entering his eighties, the creative powers of America's grand old man of architecture seemed to gather strength rather than diminish. Activity at Taliesin increased, as evidenced by the thousands of plans and sketches from these years that have been preserved in Taliesin's archives.

Unfortunately, with this deluge of work to be gotten out, the tight personal control Wright had always kept over his projects could not be maintained. Many of the houses erected during this period, in their siting, design details, and construction lacked Wright's usual care. This, apparently, was the hard price Wright paid for his newfound success.

A delightful exception to the "crank-it-out" design procedure was the house Wright did for his son David, outside of Phoenix. Some of the give-and-take between father and son during the construction of this house provides interesting insight on Wright's relationship with his children, or at least, with one of them. David, a concrete block manufacturer and, by his own description, a pretty good amateur engineer, served as general contractor for the building work. When Wright stopped by during the construction of the roof he pointed at braces between the rafters and said, "Those braces must go." Father and son locked eyes; "I don't think so," said David. And the son prevailed.

Later, when Wright tried to tear away plantings that David's wife had put in, David angrily told his father to stop. "I guess you'd rather I wasn't here," said the elder Wright. David was not moved by his father's words: "That's right," he said. Wright got into a chauffeur-driven car and rolled away.

A striking habit of Wright's in his lifetime of work—one he shared with other creative geniuses—was the way he would come back, time to time, to earlier design ideas that for one reason or another had never been completed. An example of this is found in the Price Tower (1953-1956) in Bartlesville, Oklahoma. The Tower's design is based on one that Wright originally created nearly twenty-five years earlier for the never-built apartment tower for St. Marks in the Bowerie Church, in New York City.

To someone driving toward Bartlesville today, the nineteen-story skyscraper thrusting up from the otherwise nearly featureless horizon is indeed astonishing. Most of the city's other structures are perhaps two- or three-stories high. But its uniqueness, and its bold visibility, are no accident. Wright had always argued that a skyscraper's reason for being, as a symbol of man's aspiration and individuality, is lost on the crowded streets of cities. To his way of thinking, a skyscraper was most beautiful when it was so located as to cast its own shadow and be seen from all directions. He also liked the idea of people being able to live and work in the same place, so Price Tower is actually a commercial space on the lower floors and an apartment house on the upper floors.

Completed in 1956 at a cost of about two and a half million dollars—a million dollars over budget and sixteen stories taller than the client had originally asked for—the Price Tower proved to be a big success from design, engineering, and publicity viewpoints.

As he had done with previous buildings—the Johnson Wax building, for example—Wright designed all the furniture for the Tower, and just as in that case, his chairs were terribly tippy. On one occasion the governor of Oklahoma fell to the floor off of one of Wright's chairs. Hearing about this, the architect, not in the least embarrassed, sent the following note off to Harold Price:

Dear "Hal the Great" Senior:

I learn by grapevine. . .that as your architect I got the governor down on the floor. Well, Hal, he can't be much of a governor if the poor devil can't even negotiate a Price Tower official chair?

Happy landings, always, always—

Affectionately,

Frank

As the Price Tower was nearing completion, Wright was also engaged in several religious buildings, projects for which he felt he had a special affinity. "I've always considered myself deeply religious," he told an interviewer in 1957. "I go occasionally to this [church] and then sometimes to that one, but my church—I put capital N on Nature and go there." But Wright had an extraordinary ability to grasp the central truth of religions that he initially knew little or nothing about. The outstanding example of this particular gift was demonstrated in Wright's design for the Beth Shalom synagogue in Elkins Park, Pennsylvania, a suburb of Philadelphia.

When Wright was contacted by Rabbi Mortimer Cohen about undertaking such a project, the architect expressed a great willingness to work closely with him to become familiar with the symbols and objects related to Judaism before beginning. What was wanted, the rabbi said, was a temple that expressed "a new thing—the American spirit wedded to the ancient spirit of Israel." What he got a few months later was more than the Rabbi had dared to hope for: a temple that captured the meaning and power of Mount Sinai, where God and Moses met.

Wright achieved this masterful design by creating a tent-like triangular enclosure, symbolizing both the Tabernacle, wherein the sacred texts were kept, and the mountain itself. A steel and aluminum tripod frame supports the soaring roof, its double-thick translucent roof-walls sheltering the congregation, the architect said, "as if they were resting in the very hands of God." As a place designed to bring forth the religious spirit, Beth Shalom Temple succeeded probably better in this regard than any of Wright's other houses of worship.

The Guggenheim Museum, another project of this second Golden Age at Taliesin was one of the more controversial designs Wright ever executed. Wright's connection with this project had begun when he received a note in 1943 from Hilla Rebay, an artist herself and the artistic *aide de camp* to multimillionaire Solomon R. Guggenheim. It was she who had first interested Guggenheim in abstract art, and as his collection grew to some eight hundred works, the two of them began to conceive the idea of a wonderful new museum to house them.

A woman of mystical inclinations, Rebay found Wright's spiritual way of talking about architecture consistent with her own way of thinking, and she determined that he would design their new art institution. She asked Wright to come to New York and talk things over, explaining that what was wanted was "a temple of spirit—a monument, and your help to make it possible." The meeting went well, and after a number of months he sent Rebay a letter proposing a radical design based upon an open circular court and a spiral ramp leading from top to bottom. He described it this way:

> A museum should be one extended expansive well-proportioned floor space from bottom to top. . . . No stops anywhere and such screened divisions of the space gloriously lit within from above, as would deal appropriately with every group of paintings or individual paintings as you might want them classified.
>
> The atmosphere of the whole should be luminous from bright to dark, anywhere desired: a great calm and breadth pervading the whole place. . . .
>
> In short a creation which does not yet exist.

Rebay and Guggenheim, at first enthusiastic about Wright's proposals, began to have doubts as friends who saw his sketches expressed concerns about the revolutionary design ideas. But after the usual exchange of letters, most of them strongly worded scoldings from Wright, the uneasy clients fell into line. The project was delayed for several years thereafter, but it was eventually resumed in 1956.

Wright's disdain for "the neighbors" of one of his creations—that is to say, the buildings around it—is particularly evident where the Guggenheim Museum is concerned. Most contemporary architects keep the surrounding architecture in mind when they design a structure, in an effort to achieve a harmonious effect. But Wright apparently thought that his own works were strong enough to create their own surroundings.

The Guggenheim presents a dramatic sculptural form when viewed from the outside. Inside it offers an ascending spiral ramp that creates a continuous display area for art. The overall effect is powerful, even dazzling. Unfortunately, many painters and sculptors do not find it attractive. When the design was published, hundreds of them protested that a curved wall and a sloping ceiling distracted from the rectangular forms that most paintings take. But Wright was unmoved. He answered that they would simply have to conform to "the mother art-Architecture," and that in doing so, they might even become better painters. But the complaints continued after the building was finished.

Virtually no art critic, however much they admired the building itself as a work of art, thought the Guggenheim well suited as a place in which to exhibit art, for just as the artists had feared, the Guggenheim's interior itself remains *the* most important experience for anyone entering there.

During the many years of the Guggenheim's planning and construction, including those years when all activities were on hold, Wright and his wife Olgivanna occupied a suite at New York's famous Plaza Hotel, apparently with the rent paid by Solomon Guggenheim. Wright took instantly to the celebrity-adoring city, and New York in turn instantly took to the publicity-adoring architect. He returned to the suite so often in the following years that in time it came to be known as Taliesin East.

The latter days of Wright's career were rich in both the quantity and quality of the designs that came from his drafting table, many of them done speculatively at his own expense. These included a number of public works projects—that is, buildings and other structures designed for various government agencies. Especially close to his heart was the Monona Terrace Civic Center in Madison, Wisconsin, for which Wright drew up at least three designs between 1938 and 1955.

It always rankled Wright that he had never received a commission for a building or other structure from his own home state of Wisconsin. And in this case his record remained unspoiled—he did not receive approval for his Monona Terrace plans.

Other unbuilt public works projects were his two skyscraper designs for Chicago, the Half-Mile High Building, proposed in 1933 for that city's world's fair, and the Mile-High Building that he announced in 1956 to contain all the government departments of the state of Illinois. Many engineering experts said that the upper stories of such a building would sway so much in a wind that they would be dangerous, an opinion that Wright rejected. But the argument would never be resolved, for the state of Illinois showed no interest in constructing the five-hundred-story skyscraper.

At the same press conference in which Wright revealed his Mile-High Building plans, he also displayed a list of names of men whom he respected professionally, and why. This is one of the few instances in which Wright publicly expressed admiration for anyone other than himself. The list read as follows:

Memorial To:

Louis Sullivan, son of Chicago
First made the tall building tall

Elisha Otis
Inventor of the upended street (i.e., the elevator)

John Roebling
First steel-in-tension on the grand scale:
the Brooklyn Bridge

Lidgerwood, naval architect
First ocean liner keel.
Makes it what it is today.

Coinget and Monier of France
Reinforced concrete.
The body of our modern world.

The latter decades of Wright's life were a golden period. Everything he had ever wanted—admiration from his professional peers, wide public acclaim, a loving and peaceful married life, challenging work to do—were his. And Wright did not fail to notice and greatly enjoy this happy change of fortune from earlier times. Indeed, there were those who found him just plain fun. William Zeckendorf, a real estate developer, told of meeting the aged architect and being caught entirely off guard by his engaging personality:

> Wright I met as a supposed antagonist on a TV discussion panel where I was supposed to be his meat. All I knew about Wright was that I liked his work. When my aides compiled a dossier of his speeches and writings, I discovered the man made profound good sense. As a result, during the TV show we sang in duet and had a great time. After the program, in order to further admire each other and ourselves, we went out to my place in Greenwich for dinner and a few drinks. The company was so excellent that we had a few more drinks, but in the course of maneuvering down into my wine cellar for a fresh bottle of brandy, Wright caught his heel on a step and fell, giving himself a nasty gash on the scalp. The next stop was the emergency ward of the hospital, where this fierce old man, refusing an anesthetic (he already had enough in him) sat on the operating table swinging his legs and singing bawdy songs as the intern stitched his scalp.

Astonishing to say, as Wright celebrated his ninetieth birthday in 1957, he embarked on the busiest year of his career. He received a total of forty commissions! Though his apprentices now did most of the detail work, it was still Frank Lloyd Wright who came up with the basic concepts—which was, after all, the part of the work he had always enjoyed most anyway. His daily routine included rising early, sketching for two or three hours, taking a long walk down to the drafting rooms at Hillside to see the work in progress, lunch, a nap, then a staff meeting, and so on into each night, which ended around 10 P.M.

Rarely sick, always sharp of mind, and sharper of tongue, he continued in this routine until April 4, 1959, when he complained of stomach pains and was rushed to the hospital in Phoenix, a few miles from Taliesin West. Five days later, on April 9, he died of a hemorrhage following surgery for an intestinal blockage.

His body was flown back to Spring Green, where some forty relatives and friends marched in slow procession behind his horse-drawn coffin to the tiny family burial ground.

One of his neighbors spoke for many when she said simply, "I just can't believe it. He was the kind of man you thought would live forever."

Old age never diminished Wright's creative drive. Seated here at his desk in Taliesin, he is the image of the grand master of architecture.

CONCLUSION

All told, Frank Lloyd Wright designed thousands of buildings, and of these about eight hundred were built. More than 280 of these are still standing, many of them designated as historic and artistic treasures.

Author Brendan Gill captured in words the fascinating mix of genuine magic and make-believe that Wright created in his life and his work over a long career:

> It is another Wright who flourishes today, far beyond the boundaries of his life and time. His fame multiplies at a rate that even he would find satisfactory. Admiration of his handiwork approaches the universal. Who complains any longer that his roofs leak, that his chairs draw blood, that he never used to pay his bills? Old scamp, old teller of lies, old maker of wonders! How do you manage to go on performing this feat of hypnotism upon us?. . . Again and again, a moment comes when in our imaginations we find ourselves crowing about the young-old wizard. We fall silent, sensing that something is about to happen. . . . A tray of colored pencils is at his elbow. A fire crackles upon a nearby stone hearth.
>
> We watch in awe as from a hand moving lightly and swiftly across the drafting table there leaps into being something never seen before.

In his works as in the conduct of his private life, Wright gave constant and unfaltering witness to a favorite saying of his: "Take care of the luxuries, and let the necessities take care of themselves." More than any other American architect he served people's deepest need to derive both use and pleasure from the buildings they live and work in. One cannot see or be inside of a Wright building and remain unmoved; the beauty and extravagance of his creations issue an insistent and irresistible command: "Look at me! Experience me!"

CHRONOLOGY

1825	William Cary Wright, father of Frank Lloyd Wright, born in Hartford, Connecticut.
1839	Anna Lloyd Jones, mother of Frank Lloyd Wright, born in Wales, Great Britain; comes to America in 1845.
1861	*Civil War breaks out.*
1863	*Lincoln issues the Emancipation Proclamation.*
	William ordained a Baptist minister.
1865	*End of Civil War. Lincoln assassinated.*
1866	William and Anna marry.
1867	June 8, Wright born in Richland Center, Wisconsin.
1878	After a number of relocations, Wright family moves to Madison, Wisconsin.
1885	William files for divorce from Anna. Wright quits high school.
1886	Goes to work as draftsman for William Conover, a civil engineer; begins attending classes at University of Wisconsin.
1887	Quits college, moves to Chicago, works briefly for J. Lyman Silsbee. Joins the firm of Adler & Sullivan.
1889	Marries Catherine Tobin.
1893	Sullivan fires Wright for doing extra design work at home and stealing his clients.

1894	Opens Chicago office with architect friend Cecil Corwin. Does first independent design job, the Winslow house in River Forest, Illinois.
1896	Designs "Romeo & Juliet" windmill for aunts Nell and Jane Lloyd.
1899–1909	Wright experiences great growth in his business and family; begins developing a truly American house-design concept he calls Prairie Style.
1902	Designs the Willits house, later described by a critic as "the first masterpiece among the Prairie houses."
1904	Designs and builds headquarters for Larkin Company, Darwin Martin's employer.
1905	Designs the Oak Park Unity Church. Makes first trip to Japan.
1908	Asks Catherine for a divorce; she refuses.
1909	Berlin firm, Wasmuth, publishes a portfolio of Wright's designs.
1910	Returns to United States. Anna Wright gives her son gift of land in Spring Green, Wisconsin. He designs and begins construction of a new home/workplace he calls Taliesin.
1911	Taliesin is completed. Wright closes his Oak Park office, leaves Catherine and his children and moves to Taliesin with Mamah.
1913	Wins commission to design Western-style Imperial Hotel in Tokyo. Back in Wisconsin, receives commission to design lavish Midway Gardens in Chicago.
1914	*World War I begins in Europe.* Mass murder and fire at Taliesin. Rebuilds Taliesin; Miriam Noel moves into Taliesin.
1917	*United States enters World War I.*
1918	*Germany surrenders in November.*
1922	Catherine grants Wright a divorce.

1923	*Earthquake in Japan, hotel undamaged.* Anna Wright dies. He marries Miriam Noel. Five months later, she leaves him.
1925	Taliesin is badly burned again.
1927	Miriam Noel gives him a divorce.
1928	Bank takes title to Taliesin. Wright's personal effects at Taliesin are auctioned off. He marries Olgivanna Hinzenberg.
1929	*October 24, stock market crashes and the Great Depression begins.* A group of Wright's wealthy friends fund a private corporation called Wright, Incorporated, that pays off his debts and buys back Taliesin for him.
1930–1932	Wright pens his autobiography. The Taliesin Fellowship begins its program with twenty-three apprentices.
1935	Designs and exhibits Broadacre City, his utopian city of the future.
1936	Commissioned by Edgar Kaufmann, Sr., to design a country house, Wright creates his famous Fallingwater. Commissioned by Herbert Johnson to design new headquarters for Johnson's Wax Corporation.
1937	Designs and builds Taliesin West near Phoenix, Arizona. Designs his first Usonian-style house, the Jacobs house, in Madison, Wisconsin.
1939	*World War II begins in Europe.*
1941	*America enters World War II.*
1945	*Germany surrenders in May, Japan in August.*
1957	Turns ninety years old. Receives forty commissions in one year.
1959	April 9, Wright dies. Guggenheim Museum completed and dedicated after his death.

GLOSSARY

apprentice A little-trained or untrained person who works with a well-trained, experienced professional to learn a trade or craft.

architect A person who designs and supervises the consruction of buildings and other structures.

cantilever A horizontal beam held down at one end and supported near the middle, with the other end projecting out into space.

civil engineer A person who designs and supervises the construction of public works, such as bridges and roads.

column A vertical post that holds up a ceiling, floor, or roof.

commission The assignment from a customer who hires an architect to design a building or other structure.

contractor A specialist hired to perform some part of the actual construction project.

cornice A decorative piece above a doorway, window, or at a roof's edge.

detailing Sketching of the finishing ornamental details of a design, a job often turned over to an architect's assistants.

draftsman A person who carefully draws up measured plans or bleuprints for use in construction, from the ideas thought up by the architect.

eave The edge of the roof that extends out beyond the walls.

footings The earth-bound posts or concrete walls on which a building stands.

foundation See "footings."

framework The structural parts of a building that hold up the roof and walls.

modular Parts that are designed according to a standard measure so that they fit together perfectly.

parapet Low wall, rail, or mound along the edge of a platform, balcony, or roof.

post-and-beam Post: vertical-support structure; beam: horizontal-support structure, held up by posts. Together they make up the traditional method of construction used from ancient times to the present.

reinforced concrete Poured concrete that has many steel rods woven together inside the concrete to give it added strength.

skylight A window in the roof that lets light enter from above.

skyscraper A tall building, ten stories or more.

structure Any kind of work done by a builder that rises above the ground: house, skyscraper, bridge, coliseum, factory, etc.

terrace A balcony or deck.

utilities In a building, the plumbing, heating, electricity, ventilation systems.

BIBLIOGRAPHY

Condit, Carl W. *The Chicago School of Architecture.* Chicago: University of Chicago Press, 1964.

Bolon, Carol, ed. *The Nature of Frank Lloyd Wright.* Chicago: University of Chicago.

Fitch, James Marston. *The American Building.* London, England: B. T. Batsford, 1948.

Gideon, S. *Space, Time and Architecture,* 3rd ed. New York: Cambridge University Press, 1956.

Gill, Brendan. *Many Masks: A Life of Frank Lloyd Wright.* New York: G. P. Putnam, 1987.

Gowans, Alan. *Images of American Living.* Philadelphia: J. B. Lippincott, 1964.

Hitchcock, Henry-Russell. *In the Nature of Materials, Buildings of Frank Lloyd Wright,* 1887-1941. New York: Duell, Sloan, 1942.

Kemp, Jim. *American Vernacular.* New York: Viking Press, 1987.

Scott, Margaret Helen. *Frank Lloyd Wright's Warehouse.* Richland, Wisconsin: Richland Center, 1984.

Scully, Vincent. *Modern Architecture.* New York: George Braziller, 1961.

Smith, G. E. Kidder. *A Pictorial History of Architecture in America.* Boston: American Heritage, 1976.

Storrer, William Allen. *Catalog of Frank Lloyd Wright Buildings.* Boston: MIT Press, 1974.

Twombly, Robert C. *Frank Lloyd Wright: An Interpretive Biography.* New York: Harper & Row, 1973.

Wright, Frank Lloyd. *Letters to Architects,* B. B. Pfieffer, ed. Fresno, California: California State University at Fresno, 1984.

Wright, Frank Lloyd. *Letters to Apprentices,* B. B. Pfieffer, ed. Fresno, California: California State University at Fresno, 1977.

Wright, Frank Lloyd. *Letters to Clients,* B. B. Pfieffer, ed. Fresno, California: California State University at Fresno, 1986.

INDEX

Photo Credits:

Cover: Pedro E. Guerrero; **Cover Insert:** Ezra Stoller/ Esto. **Frontispiece:** Pedro E. Guerro; Pages 11 left and right, 99: Courtesy Frank Lloyd Wright Foundation; 15: University of Wisconsin-Madison; 22: Chicago Historical Society; 28: Historical Pictures Service; 35: The Oak Park Public Library; 37: Pedro E. Guerro; 40: The Buffalo and Erie County Historical Society; 44, 64, 71, 92: UPI/ Bettman Newsphotos; 54: Phil H. Fedderson; 58: TSW-Click/ Chicago; 74: Spencer Grant/ Photo Researchers; 83: AP/ Wide World; 86: The Bettman Archive; 94: Courtesy Johnson Wax; 103: Ralph Krubner/ Black Star; 106: George Cserna;118: The FLW Archives. **Color Insert:** Page 1: Marvin Konar/ Black Star; 2: Deckart/ Leo de Wys; 3: The Metropolitan Museum of Art, Purchase, 1967, Edward C. Moore, Jr. Gift and Edgar J. Kaufman Charitable Foundation Gift; 4, 5: Courtesy Frank Lloyd Wright Foundation; 6: Restricted gift of Mrs. Theodore D. Tieken, 1976.61G, © 1989 The Art Institute of Chicago. All Rights Reserved; 7, 8: Ezra Stoller/ Esto.

Photo Research: Photosearch Inc.

DATE DUE			

 GUMi